THE TECHNOLOGY OF JOURNALISM

Medill School of Journalism
VISIONS *of the* AMERICAN PRESS

GENERAL EDITOR
David Abrahamson

THE TECHNOLOGY
OF JOURNALISM
CULTURAL AGENTS,
CULTURAL ICONS

Patricia L. Dooley

Foreword by Neil Chase

MEDILL SCHOOL OF JOURNALISM

Northwestern University Press
Evanston, Illinois

Northwestern University Press
www.nupress.northwestern.edu

Printed in the United States of America

10 9 8 7 6 5 4 3 2 1

ISBN-13: 978-0-8101-2330-4
ISBN-10: 0-8101-2330-4

Library of Congress Cataloging-in-Publication Data

Dooley, Patricia L.
  The technology of journalism : cultural agents, cultural icons /
Patricia L. Dooley ;
 foreword by Neil Chase.
      p. cm. — (Visions of the American press)
  Includes bibliographical references and index.
  ISBN-13: 978-0-8101-2330-4 (pbk. : alk. paper)
  ISBN-10: 0-8101-2330-4 (pbk. : alk. paper)
  1. Journalism—Technological innovations. 2. Journalism—History.
I. Title. II. Series.
PN4784.T34D66 2007
070.40285—dc22

                                        2007026876

   ∞ The paper used in this publication meets the minimum
requirements of the American National Standard for Information
Sciences—Permanence of Paper for Printed Library Materials,
              ANSI Z39.48-1992.

To Jon and Sarah, with love

CONTENTS

FOREWORD

Neil Chase

Visit the intersection of journalism and technology, as Patricia L. Dooley suggests in this thoughtful volume, and you'll find it's not a place where two perpendicular paths cross. It more closely resembles a beehive. Innovation enters from all directions, mostly in the form of ideas and inventions not originally intended for the news business. Publishers and broadcasters reach the intersection either because they are driven there by emotions ranging from curiosity to fear to greed or because they've taken a wrong turn. When they meet, journalism finds wonderful uses for what technology has created. Sometimes, it's related to the manufacturing part of the business: a new way to distribute news faster or more cheaply, to get it to more people, or to reduce the money and time needed to cover a story or sell an ad. Often, the innovators are the journalists themselves, people who drive into that complex intersection looking for specific ways to improve the process of news gathering and delivery:

- Reporters who used carrier pigeons to send copy from European war zones and then a century later adapted satellite phones to do the same thing
- Photographers who turned hotel bathrooms into darkrooms while on out-of-town assignments
- Sportswriters who used the first portable (better described as "luggable") computers to cover games without having to return to the office or dictate over the phone

- Editors who produced a newspaper using desktop computers in a borrowed office across the street after the 1989 San Francisco earthquake crippled their newsroom and their multimillion-dollar publishing system (and the graphic artist who remembered the old technology and drew maps by hand that night)

In some of the most fascinating cases, innovative technology actually changes the nature of the storytelling. It makes the news more relevant, more approachable, more valuable, more entertaining, or easier to comprehend. That certainly happened when people figured out how to print photographs in the newspaper, packing a thousand descriptive words into a single halftone image that did a better job of telling the story. When radio news graduated from on-air reading to the use of sound recorded in the field, it brought about another worth-a-thousand-words innovation (followed, perhaps unfortunately, by allowing everyone in town to call in and rant live on the air). Television gave journalists the extraordinary ability to show the news and not just talk about it.

Those innovations were moments of major significance in the relationship between journalism and technology. They were big changes, decades apart, in the days when technology meant big machines, big decisions, and big costs. For most of the twentieth century, the intersection of journalism and technology was mainly populated by large companies. In the 1990s, the information highway department reconfigured the intersection. The commercialization of the Internet, the evolution of the World Wide Web, and the related simplification of computer programming allowed journalists to single-handedly create new forms of storytelling—sometimes within minutes. "Imagine what we could do with this," a fellow journalist said as he gave me my first glimpse at the Web in the summer of 1994. We were looking at Web pages that could tell you whether a coffeepot or a vending machine was full, but his eyes gleamed with ideas for online journalism. The story of the years after that summer could be told in terms of technology: Web pages became more sophisticated, starting with text but soon carrying photos and simple graphics, then audio, video, interactive tools, database interfaces, and much more. As Web users gained increasing amounts of processing speed on their computers and more robust connections that allowed faster access to more complicated pages, the richness of online journalism grew.

But that technology time line is overshadowed by the true paradigm change: the fascinating transition in the ways we can tell stories and the effects those stories can have. Journalism changed. Not because technology changed it but because some very innovative storytellers used that technology to make the changes happen. Consider several ways news organizations have used new tools to improve citizen participation in the operation of democracies:

- Elections are vital, but too many people abstain, while others vote without understanding the choices. In Colombia, a weekly newsmagazine prepared voters for a national election by creating an interactive "figure out which candidate you support" questionnaire on the Web: answer questions about your positions on key issues and we'll help you decide which candidate is the best match. Thousands used it, and the results collected from users ended up accurately predicting the election results. This undoubtedly brought into the process people who would have otherwise abstained.
- One story that's simultaneously crucial and incomprehensible is the annual budget. From a national government to the tiniest municipality, the budget affects every citizen. But don't expect most people to understand it. In New York City, a

small independent weekly newspaper decided to change that. So it created an interactive graphic that explained the city's budgeting process and let the reader wear the shoes of a city official. Think the city should spend more on schools? Great, but you have to take money from highway repair to do it. More cops? You can raise the police budget as much as you want, but you have to take money from other services to do so, unless you raise taxes.

• When King County, Washington, was considering a tax increase to pay for highway and transportation improvements, the *Seattle Times* built a list of all the projects being considered, the alternatives and costs for each, and the possible sources of revenue. It then let readers decide which projects should be completed and how the money should be raised. A story in the paper clearly explained the results, with more than two thousand people participating, and the voice of those readers led the local government to change its plans.

Consider also the new job descriptions for journalists. At many newspapers, "print" reporters are recording audio in the field and doing TV-like stand-up reports in front of video cameras. "Print" photographers carry hybrid still-and-video cameras and report stories differently because they're thinking of slide shows, video packages, and that big photo for page A-1. A foreign correspondent for a newspaper films a video report from the roof of a house in Baghdad. Another carries a video camera into a troubled African nation and hands it to a freelance still photographer; the two then collaborate on a compelling video report from a place the television networks have never visited. At the same time, a TV station's producer is learning to write in more of a print style for the online version of tonight's local news report. And a radio host is now shaving in the mornings because there's a live online video version of his show.

There are plenty of jokes about journalists as dinosaurs, about reporters who can't use a computer because they can't find the carriage-return lever, about the need for one journalist to change the lightbulb while another twenty-four reminisce about how great the old one was and how there was no need to replace it so quickly just because it burned out. But in today's newsrooms, it's the journalists who are leading the change. They're writing quick versions of stories for the Web during the day; some say that focusing on a lead before lunchtime helps them shape their ideas and determine the lines of reporting for the rest of the day or week for the final version.

Perhaps the biggest surprise to traditional news professionals is that evolving technology has even changed the sources of news. When a well-known celebrity died recently, an editor at a major U.S. newspaper saw it on the Web site Wikipedia within a minute of the first news report. "How'd they get that so fast?" he asked. He pictured a central Wikipedia newsroom monitoring the headlines and posting information. But he didn't understand that Wikipedia is the result of collaboration by millions of people. Professional editors and academics are quick to dismiss Wikipedia because the information on its pages can be easily changed and is not subjected to the kind of fact-checking that is done in traditional newsrooms. But of course, the millions of users will tell you they understand where the information comes from and have the intelligence to evaluate it themselves.

When a breaking news event affects a large area or happens out of the sight of news cameras, amateur photographers provide the still and video images that the world sees. Have a hunch about a story but no evidence? Put a note in the paper and on the Web site, and readers will join in the journalism. Post original documents on the Web when you run an important story so that readers will know more about how you did the reporting, but don't be surprised when they raise additional questions about the story or correct it. Thousands of people now identify themselves as journalists without having a press pass from a corporate institution. Is that blogger for a community Web site sitting next to you in the press gallery at a city council meeting also a journalist? Absolutely. And that's hard for some old-fashioned journalists to swallow.

So the intersection of journalism and technology has certainly changed the content, speed, and formats of news. But the most profound effect has been on journalists themselves. The most creative ones, the innovators, have become leaders at a time when the industry desperately needs their guidance. Those who care passionately about the responsibility of journalism to bring sunshine to the dark areas of government and democracy are finding more ways to do it and feel that they're more effective than ever. People who collect and disseminate news without the standard journalism degree or a career of hopping from tiny news outlets to progressively larger ones are getting their work read, seen, and respected.

Those who resist change and worship burned-out filaments are now rushing to catch up with the leaders, the ones who had that "imagine what we can do" gleam when they first saw new technology. And that's why—when one considers the historical past of journalism and technology, as Professor Dooley so ably does in this work—the future of journalism is exciting, not gloomy. When the whole industry reaches the intersection and decides which way to turn, just imagine what we can do. It's enough to put a gleam in your eye.

All of us who learned to type on a typewriter can probably remember what it felt like when we switched to our first word processor. For me, it was in 1986 when I began writing my master's thesis. As I started on my old IBM Selectric, I wondered if I would finish by the end of the semester. Hearing of my predicament, a friend invited me to look at a machine she had just purchased for roughly $2,000—"the Amazing Kaypro II."[1] A few days later, after visits to my bank's loan department and a little computer store in a former Chinese restaurant, I headed home with my first personal computer (PC). There would be no turning back: I had entered the computer age.

Encased in its metal box, the twenty-six-pound machine with 64K of random access memory (RAM) looked more like a portable sewing machine than anything else. But gazing at my new Kaypro, with its detachable keyboard, nine-inch "Monster Monitor," and two high-density, 180K floppy drives, I began to gain hope that I would finish on deadline after all. Five weeks later, after printing the last page of my thesis, I threw away my typewriter, carbon paper, and correction fluid. Writing and editing on the Kaypro's little black-and-green screen was so much easier that the future seemed full of new possibilities.

Twenty years later, the positive impact my first PC had on my thesis-writing experience came to mind as I prepared to teach a class on the history and theory of communication at Wichita State

University's Elliott School of Communication. The course studies the role of technologies in the communication process, and we look particularly at journalism as we discuss technological determinism, social determinism, media ecology, and actor-network theory.

When asked to think about the implications of technology on the history of journalism, students can always quickly identify examples: the printing press led to the replacement of the town crier; the telegraph led to cooperative news gathering and eventually radio and television news; the halftone and handheld camera led to the blossoming of photojournalism. But as we discuss the roles the audience and contextual conditions play in the process of change in journalism, they begin to understand that to give technology sole possession of anything as complex as journalism is unwise.

Considering that we are experiencing what many are calling a digital revolution, I consider this to be an excellent time for the publication of a book on the question of technology's role in the history of journalism. But as I started the project, I knew it would be a challenging one. What has been written about the history of journalism has often been couched in the discourse of technological determinism. In response, critics have warned against the threat of being overly charmed by the capabilities of technologies. British historian and social theorist Raymond Williams wrote that the idea of technological determinism was one of the twentieth century's most prevailing and harmful myths. American communication scholar James W. Carey has warned journalism historians to guard against the dangers of hyperbole and oversimplification in their accounts of the history of journalism.

This book synthesizes the scholarship that has been published on the historical intersection between technology and journalism.

For three hundred years, American journalism has been affected by technology, but embedded in this process of change are social, cultural, and other forces that should not be ignored. After chapter 1's review of what historians have written on the role of technology in the history of news, chapter 2 defines the technologies of journalism and gives an account of how the printing press, telegraph, still and motion picture camera, radio, television, and computer came to be used for the dissemination of news. Chapter 3 discusses a variety of nontechnological forces that have impacted the news, and chapter 4 studies the nineteenth-century phenomenon of "more and more news." Chapter 5 investigates the role of human agency in the process of change in journalism, and chapters 6 through 8 explore in greater detail journalists' adoption of electrical, visual, and computer technologies. The idea of the "press as symbol" is introduced in chapter 9, which considers how the American press became connected to the country's core cultural values, such as freedom, valor, perseverance, and Yankee ingenuity. The book's concluding chapter discusses the future of print in the context of today's emerging blogosphere and other developments.

I would like to thank David Abrahamson and Northwestern University Press for the opportunity to contribute to their series of books on the history of journalism. My husband, Jon Walstrom, has once again blessed me with his astute advice and wonderful support, and thanks go to my daughter, Sarah, for her unreserved confidence in me. My grandchildren and students have taught me about the roles communication technologies play in the lives of today's younger generations. My colleagues at the Elliott School of Communication, particularly Susan Huxman and Keith Williamson, have been a great source of comfort through this process. And special thanks go to my Elliott School colleague, coauthor, and friend Les Anderson, whose support and knowledge of journalism I have depended on. Professor Anderson and I worked together on several research papers that he generously allowed me to rely on for this book.

PATRICIA L. DOOLEY

ONE

================◇================

INTRODUCTION

History tells us that technologies have led to significant changes in journalism. In the mid-nineteenth century, the telegraph allowed news publishers to gather and send news with great speed because they had been freed from the constraints of previous communication systems. By early in the twentieth century, the camera's power to create photographic images of people and events that readers could not view firsthand was being captured by those involved in the early development of the field of photojournalism. And today, people without formal ties to the news professions are discovering that blogging software can help them become journalists in an instant.

By the same token, however, humans have shared news throughout much of history without the aid of printing presses or the other technologies associated with journalism. Titus Livius, whose lifework was the *History of Rome,* wrote of news criers in his chronicling of the city's story from its founding in 753 B.C. until the time of Drusus in 9 B.C. Human runners were used to convey news in ancient times over vast expanses of territory. Starting around 1200, news was spread throughout continental Europe,

1

England, and Scandinavia by balladeers singing about the events of the times in poetic form. After Johannes Gutenberg's mid-fifteenth-century printing press ushered in its revolutionary new world, it would take more than one hundred years before sheets resembling what we think of today as newspapers were printed. Even now, in a world awash in mediated forms of news, we still often hear about important events from our friends, families, and acquaintances.

That people have not always been quick to replace extant tools and techniques should remind us to be circumspect in our assessments of how technologies have affected journalism. Yet the tantalizing promise of new technology has often been difficult to resist. Popular histories of the telegraph typically relate the story of Samuel F. B. Morse's recognition that his new machine would change the world: in the first public demonstration of his telegraph, in 1844, he sent the message "What hath God wrought?" In a discussion of the power of the camera, art critic Walter Benjamin declared that it "introduces us to unconscious optics as does psychoanalysis to unconscious impulses." Reflecting on the wonders of radio in a poem, Josephine Preston Peabody wrote: "This is a marvel of the universe: to fling a thought across a stretch of sky." About television journalism, Fred Friendly stated: "TV is bigger than any story it reports. It's the greatest teaching tool since the printing press." And in 1948, Norbert Wiener, who popularized the social implications of cybernetics, wrote that he hoped the era's new information technologies would prevent humanity from plunging us back into "the world of Belsen and Hiroshima."[3]

How have writers on the history of journalism regarded technology in their analyses of the dynamics of change in the field? While historians have published works on particular technologies —and many have published works on the history of journalism—

relatively few have focused on the intersection of technology and journalism. An examination of the scholarship on the history of journalism reveals a bias that favors technology as a driving force behind changes in news, especially among the field's earliest historians. A tendency to equate journalism with its technologies, for example, is seen in the common use of the term *the press* after Gutenberg's mid-1400s invention began to spread rapidly throughout continental Europe and eventually to England and the New World. As telegraphic, photographic, broadcasting, computer, and Internet technologies have been adopted by journalists, historians have divided the field into the eras of print, broadcasting, visual, and digital journalism. Their many references to the "rise" and "spread" of journalism's technologies convey the idea that technologies have a natural tendency to grow and move through society on their own.[4] And historians who favor technologies tend to valorize those individuals who are most obviously associated with them, rendering the roles of others involved in the process of change in journalism less visible.

America's first well-known journalism historian was the American Revolutionary War–era printer Isaiah Thomas. In 1810, having dedicated himself to memorializing the machine that helped his new country win its freedom from the British, he published a massive tome titled *The History of Printing in America*.[5] Thomas's book offered a detailed rendition of the emergence and development of the nation's printing and newspaper industries in the seventeenth and eighteenth centuries.

Having risked his life to free America from British control, Thomas was in an ideal position to document the contributions of the press and members of his craft to its newfound freedom. And after the war, he witnessed how the enhanced stature of both the press and its products led to a rapid growth in the number and influence of newspapers. In retrospect, he wrote: "To an observer of the great utility of the kind of publications called newspapers, it may appear strange that they should have arisen to the present almost incredible number, from a comparatively late beginning." With hopes of pleasing the period's "professional men," Thomas also acknowledged the pivotal role printing presses and those who operated them played in the early history of American journalism.[6]

Thomas's history was the standard text in the field until mid-century, when other retired journalists published histories of the newspaper. Joseph Tinker Buckingham (1779–1861), a prolific writer, editor, and publisher who was involved with both newspapers and magazines, published two sets of books on the newspaper business after he retired. Filled with personal stories and commentary on important papers and their publishers and editors, Buckingham's books focused largely on the newspapers published in New England and the mid-Atlantic states. He characterized the history of the printing press and newspaper as a march of progress and its printers and editors as heroes.[7]

In 1873, former *New York Herald* managing editor Fredrick Hudson published America's next major history of journalism. Hudson explained in the 789-page book's preface that his was the first complete treatment of the history of the American press. Over the course of his career, he witnessed the introduction of the telegraph to the world of news publishing. As he prepared for retirement, pondering the role of technology and other factors in the process of change in journalism, he wrote:

> All created things have an origin. Where there is a necessity in a community, some one supplies the want. . . . When ideas, and signs, and words came, something was necessary to put words

into shape to communicate ideas with greater rapidity. Type were [sic] invented for this purpose. Ink and rude presses came with type, as gutta-percha with the telegraph. Written news-slips were too slowly prepared even for the slow age of Gutenburg and Schœffer. Newspapers, therefore, became a necessity, and were invented in their turn. Then came steam and electricity as auxiliary powers to intellect. What next? The pneumatic tunnel—the universal newspaper carrier![8]

Despite his stated sentiment that necessity is the mother of invention, he filled his history of American journalism with references to the transformative power of the telegraph and new devices adopted by newspeople over the course of his career.

Using the histories produced by Thomas, Buckingham, and Hudson as models, a raft of writers produced books documenting the histories of the presses of their communities on local, county, and state levels.[9] In addition, several books were published that provided statistics on the establishment of the printing press and newspapers across the United States and other countries since the first papers were started. One of the earliest of these compilations, published by W. T. Coggeshall in 1857, included a large amount of data on not only American newspapers but also papers across the world since the earliest of them started appearing in the seventeenth century. The U.S. Census Bureau published two similar compendiums, one by S. N. D. North in 1884 and a second by William S. Rossiter in 1900. Such books characterized the printing press and newspapers as precipitators of progress of a powerful nature. Other than identifying the printers and editors who managed the presses, the authors of these volumes paid little attention to emerging technologies or other factors that affected the newspaper business.[10]

Beginning in the early twentieth century, similar compilations of information about printing and newspapers were published by bibliographers who sought to document as many aspects of the fields of printing and news publishing as possible. The most prolific of these scholars was Douglas C. McMurtrie (1888–1944), who published dozens of works on printing and newspapers. From a book on the Gutenberg press to a history of the products of Chicago's first printing presses, McMurtrie spared no praise for the capabilities of these presses and those who operated them both in the broader field of publishing and within the journalistic industry itself.

McMurtrie was part of a generation of journalists and scholars who contributed to a late-nineteenth-century movement to establish university and college courses devoted to teaching students how to become professional news reporters and editors. Among the nation's oldest news education courses were those started in the early 1890s at the University of Kansas and Indiana University. As the rest of the country's colleges and universities followed in the footsteps of these educational leaders and set up their own journalism programs, more histories of journalism and other instructional materials were published. Some of the authors of these works were more prone than their nineteenth-century counterparts to look at the roles of social, cultural, economic, and geographic factors in their interpretations of the field's history. Nevertheless, they still exhibited a healthy regard for the power of the press and those who operated it.

Among the best known of these textbooks is Willard Grosvenor Bleyer's 1927 *Main Currents in the History of American Journalism*. Bleyer started by telling his readers that he would help them "understand the present-day American newspaper and its problems" by providing them with "an historical background sufficient for an intelligent understanding of the American newspaper of today."[11] His concluding chapter focused on how the newspaper industry of the 1920s was "profoundly influenced in its development" by the "tremendous mechanical progress" of the previous twenty-five years. He wrote:

> The age was one of machinery. Ingenious machines were devised to do practically everything that had previously been done by hand. Mechanical inventions and improvements were as important in newspaper production as they were in other fields. The modern newspaper would have been impossible without huge perfecting presses, the linotype, the autoplate, color printing, and the half-tone and rotogravure processes. Other inventions that were of great value to newspapers were the telephone, the typewriter, radio communication, the telegraph printing machine, and the automobile. From one point of view, the present-day newspaper is a machine-made product to a greater extent than ever before.[12]

Machines, according to Bleyer, were responsible for changes in journalism such as increased speed and efficiency of printing, rising circulations, and faster transmission of news. "Newspapers very naturally took advantage of every improvement in communication and transportation," he observed.[13] In addition, Bleyer credited technology with triggering industrial developments that in turn led to more standardization among America's newspapers. Such industrial developments, he pointed out, included newspaper syndicates, press associations, and local press bureaus.

But while Bleyer gave considerable credit to technology, he counted societal and cultural conditions among the precipitators of change in journalism. The growth of cities, the influx of immigrants, and the rapid pace and high nervous tension "every-where manifested in American urban life" had led to the way news was written, organized, and displayed in newspapers. According to Bleyer, America's development of "big business enterprise" led newspapers to grow not only in size but also in bureaucratic complexity. And society's "various movements for higher ethical standards in business and the professions" brought new pressure on advertisers and newspaper publishers and editors to develop more socially responsible enterprises.[14]

Similar to Bleyer, Walter Lippmann and Robert E. Park, in important essays on the dynamics of change in the field of journalism, discounted the idea that technology should be given much weight. But in contrast to Bleyer, who had written of the close relationships between the newspaper and broader contextual developments, Lippmann and Park argued the newspaper was an institution largely free from the control or influence of society. In a 1925 essay titled "The Natural History of the Newspaper," Park explained: "The newspaper, like the modern city, is not wholly a national product. No one sought to make it just what it is. In spite of all the efforts of individual men and generations of men to control it and to make it something after their own heart, it has continued to grow and change in its own incalculable ways."[15] And in a 1931 essay published in the *Yale Review,* Lippmann offered a similar view in a discussion of the growing independence of newspaper from government and political parties.[16] Neither spoke directly to questions of the impact of technologies versus the impact of society on journalism.

One of the best-known twentieth-century historians of American journalism was Frank Luther Mott, who wrote, edited, or contributed to more than thirty books during his academic career at universities in Iowa and Missouri. His 1941 book, *American Jour-*

nalism, which was the field's preeminent textbook until the 1970s, went through three revisions.[17] A great admirer of journalism, Mott paid ample attention to technology and largely credited it for helping the press achieve even greater heights. His work has been criticized for being overly simplistic and too admiring of journalism. William David Sloan noted: "[For Mott] history became simply the story of the progress of journalism. . . . The past was less important for itself than for how it had contributed to the development of what journalism was to become."[18]

Edwin Emery and Henry Smith, in a 1954 textbook titled *The Press in America,* diverged to some extent from the earlier journalism historians who gave considerable power to technology in their discussions of the dynamics of change in journalism. The authors briefly mentioned the invention of the printing press in the book's opening chapter and later discussed the emergence of the telegraph and subsequent technologies. But throughout these discussions, they elevated the status of political, social, and commercial conditions among the forces that impacted the news and its associated industries. Particularly attentive to the press's role in helping people fight class struggles from the American Revolution on, they portrayed technologies as important when they helped leaders of progressive movements gain legitimacy. Revised and republished eight times, *The Press in America* was the field's major history textbook for three decades.[19]

Since the telegraph, photograph, movie, radio, and television were not invented specifically for news purposes, they did not attract the attention of press historians until after general histories on them had been published.[20] The telegraph was unveiled by Samuel Morse in 1844 and was first used for news gathering two years later. Brief reports on the use of the telegraph for news were seen as early as 1860, and one of the first in-depth accounts of the use of telegraphy in the news business was Fredrick Hudson's history of American journalism, published in 1873.[21] Hudson devoted considerable space to an account of the first uses of the telegraph by newspaper people. As one of the founding members of the Associated Press (AP), Hudson was especially knowledgeable about how telegraphy became part of the news business. In the opening of a chapter called the "Telegraphic Era," he stated: "Morse has been a benefactor of the Press. This, it is true, is not the opinion of every publisher . . . but newspaper statistics prove our position. Morse has undoubtedly struck . . . many newspapers off the lists of journalism, yet he has added many others, and increased newspaper enterprise and newspaper readers by the thousands. He has placed an electric force in every printing-office in the land."[22]

The introduction of photography in 1839 eventually led to the adoption of the photograph as a staple of the news business, but not until after the invention of the halftone would this be possible. In 1880, using Frederic Ives's new halftone technology, newspapers began publishing photos for experimental purposes. By the end of the century, photos had become a fixture in the news business. Despite the publication of several histories of illustrated newspapers in the late nineteenth century, however, scholarship on the emergence and development of the field of photojournalism did not appear until well into the twentieth century.[23]

Motion pictures, which were developed simultaneously in the 1890s in France, England, and the United States, were first used for entertainment. But in 1911, production companies around the world began using film for news dissemination after Charles Pathé was successful in doing so in France. Some journalism historians have ignored the popular newsreel. Willard Grosvenor Bleyer, for example, did not mention it in his 1927 history of journalism.

Today, Raymond Fielding's 1972 book, *The American Newsreel, 1911–1972,* is considered by many to be the standard history of the medium.[24]

Like their predecessors in the areas of telegraphic and photographic technologies, early historians of radio and television news were concerned with recounting who invented and first used these technologies for news dissemination. But since the 1960s, a fresh perspective on the impact of technology has emerged among a new group of scholars. Today, the members of this group are referred to as media ecologists, and Canadian scholar Marshall McLuhan is widely considered the father of this field of study. In his seminal 1964 book, *Understanding Media,* McLuhan proposed that the media themselves, not the content they carry, should be the focus of study. His well-known comment that "the medium is the *message*" suggests a communication medium affects society not by the content it delivers but through its unique characteristics.[25] McLuhan posited that a lightbulb is the clearest demonstration of this concept. Although it carries no content, it creates space; that is, a lightbulb creates spaces at nighttime that would otherwise be enveloped by darkness. According to McLuhan: "A light bulb creates an environment by its mere presence." He also postulated that book and newspaper content has little effect on society. He maintained that it does not matter what stories, headlines, or advertisements are in a newspaper—the effects of all newspapers are identical in that they create environments that essentially become extensions of human beings.

Well-known proponents of media ecology include Neil Postman, Walter Ong, Lewis Mumford, Jacques Ellul, Eric Havelock, Susanne Langer, Erving Goffman, and Edward T. Hall. At New York University in 1971, Postman founded the first university media ecology program. He wrote that students in the program studied "how media of communication affect human perception, understanding, feeling, and value; and how our interaction with media facilitates or impedes our chances of survival. The word ecology implies the study of environments: their structure, content, and impact on people."[26]

In a prominent study on the emergence and impact of the telegraph, James W. Carey suggested the invention altered humans' perception of space and time, a hypothesis in line with the perspectives of media ecologists.[27] The telegraph's continuous provision of messages meant people no longer were forced to wait for the news to arrive on the next stagecoach or train. Instead, news could arrive at any time. Carey posited that such a change in expectation altered the way people experienced time. In a similar vein, he proposed that the telegraph's ability to wipe out distance affected their sense of what was and was not geographically remote. No longer did the number of miles between two points matter as much as it had in the past; what was important was whether one was reachable by telegraph or some other form of communication technology.[28] Ironically, Carey was among a group who warned against overstating the power of communication technologies. In 1970, he and John J. Quirk cautioned that emerging technologies did not necessarily offer a "radical discontinuity from history and the present human condition."[29] Carey further advised historians to view technologies simply as tools to be used or not in their various endeavors.

Also in the 1970s, British scholar Raymond Williams argued against that period's preoccupation with the power of communication technologies. In a series of influential books, he rejected any form of technologically deterministic thinking that insists technologies have a life of their own and that, by itself, any form of communication technology predetermines a particular social response. Thus, to understand communication media, he said, one must analyze them within broader social, cultural, political, and economic contexts. Williams discarded the idea that humans have no agency, for if the medium really is the message, he asked, what is left for people to do or say? But even as he denounced technological determinism, he also warned: "We must be careful not to substitute for it the notion of a determined technology. Technological determinism is an untenable notion because it substitutes for real social, political and economic intention, either the random autonomy of invention or an abstract human essence. But the notion of a determined technology has a similar one-sided, one-way version of human process."[30]

A 1978 study of the history of the American newspaper sparked further interest in the question of technology's role in changes in news. In *Discovering the News,* Michael Schudson rejected technology as the chief precipitator of the penny press phenomenon of the 1830s. After describing what he viewed as the revolutionary birth of the modern press, he commented on the role of technology: "The technological argument is the powerful idea that technological advances in printing and related industries and the development of railroad transportation and later telegraphic communications were the necessary preconditions for a cheap, mass-circulation, news-hungry, and independent press."[31] While acknowledging the obvious connections of some of the changes in newspapers to improvements in technologies, Schudson dismissed the idea that technology was the most vital dynamic in this process. He wrote: "They [technologies] obviously facilitated the rise of the penny press. But they do not explain it. Technological change was not autonomous and itself begs explanation. And while it made mass circulation newspapers possible, it did not make them necessary or inevitable."[32]

In the midst of what is typically referred to as the age of new media, recent books and articles on the link between technology and the news are offering fresh interpretations of this historical relationship. A 1994 book by Menahem Blondheim studied the telegraph, the news, and their related industries from 1844 to 1897. Blondheim did not take a technologically deterministic position in his study. Instead, he integrated discussions of the roles of the public, politics, and the decision making of industry leaders into his analysis of the telegraph's impact.[33]

In an analysis of the emergence of radio news in the 1920s and 1930s, published in 1995, Gwenyth L. Jackaway investigated the competitive war between leaders in the radio and newspaper industries.[34] She argued that anytime a new technology emerges with journalistic potential, members of the old guard will resist the process with whatever weapons they can muster. When radio news began to attract advertisers, newspaper owners decided they would not share the tremendous news-gathering power they had amassed over the past hundred years in the Associated Press. Jackaway's book followed close on the heels of a book on the same topic by Robert W. McChesney, published in 1994.[35] McChesney's emphasis was on whether the American public generally supported radio or whether, by contrast, there was any organized resistance to its growth.

Kevin G. Barnhurst and John Nerone, the authors of a recent history on the forms mainstream newspapers have taken from the colonial era to 2001, factored communication technologies into their interpretation of the process of change in journalism. Eschewing technologically deterministic thinking, they argued that technologies are "only one element in a dialectical process that includes many others: economies, cultural values, political movements, the distribution of social power, and so on."[36] They defined form as "the things that make the *New York Times,* for example, recognizable as the same newspaper day after day although its content changes."[37] Examples of form include styles of writing, layout, typography, use of space, and use of pictures. Critical of previous historians' "piecemeal" approach, Barnhurst and Nerone employed a more ecological approach in which technological and news forms were paired within an emerging democratic civic culture.

Looking at the online environment in a study published in 2004, sociologist Pablo J. Boczkowski sought to understand whether already established newspapers were willing to give in to what some were saying was the wave of the future. In *Digitizing the News,* Boczkowski began by explaining his view that understanding radical change in news media required an examination of the "more evolutionary processes whereby they may or may not arise."[38] In a careful look at the online environment within several newspapers, he studied not just the roles of editors and reporters in the process of change but also the roles of others with agency in this process. His book offered a rich and nuanced account of the ways the owners of extant journalistic media react to new technologies.

In his 2005 book on the "new media" of late-seventeenth-century and early-eighteenth-century Great Britain, British historian Mark Knights demonstrated a belief in society's ability to foster the development of structures of authority for the production and distribution of knowledge, information, and opinion. According to Knights, what created the period's new pamphlets and periodicals was a combination of the printing press, the relaxation of government censorship and licensing regimes, political unrest, and urbanization. Knights counted one of the most famous of the period's pamphleteers, Daniel Defoe, as among history's first "modern" journalists.[39]

Today's trend toward globalization is having an impact on the way scholars view the relationship between technology and journalism. Concerns about globalization were present much earlier in history, but not until the past several decades have international comparative studies of developments in news begun to proliferate. Technology expert Anthony Smith has published a number of works on the international histories of newspapers and television.[40] And Mitchell Stephens covered the history of news more generally in a book following it from the "drum to the satellite." Stephens stated that changes in news have not come solely from technology, although he added that change was "facilitated by a series of technological developments."[41]

Why should any of this matter to those not involved in formal studies on the history of journalism? It is always important to consider the role of technology in journalism, but today's changing media environment brings a sense of new urgency to this concern. Whether we think much about mass media or not, everyone is vitally connected to the decisions journalists make about whether and/or how to employ the latest technologies. Journalists and technologies do not exist in a vacuum, and being well informed about journalism's historical relationship to technology puts us in a better position to be fully engaged in the construction of a better future.

Many contemporary writers portray the Internet as a revolutionary power that is wiping away the past as it reinvents the future. The Internet's creators and technical experts are among this group. Vint Cerf, regarded by many as one of the Internet's founding fathers, has written extensively about this new technology. On behalf of the Internet Society, he published a memo in 2002 titled "The Internet Is for Everyone." According to Cerf: "The Internet is proving to be one of the most powerful amplifiers of speech ever invented. It offers a global megaphone for voices that might otherwise be heard only feebly, if at all. It invites and facilitates multiple points of view and dialog in ways unimplementable by the traditional, one-way, mass media."[42]

In a book on the origins of the Internet, engineering professor John Naughton commented: "The Internet is one of the most remarkable things human beings have ever made. In terms of its impact on society, it ranks with print, the railways, the telegraph, the automobile, electric power and television. Some would equate it with print and television, the two earlier technologies that most transformed the communications environment in which people live. Yet it is potentially more powerful than both because it harnesses the intellectual leverage which print gave to mankind without being hobbled by the one-to-many nature of broadcast television."[43]

Popular culture echoes the revolution-laden rhetoric of such experts. Self-help author Dan Millman said: "I have an almost religious zeal . . . for the Internet, which is for me, the nervous system of mother Earth."[44] Likewise, heads of the world's news organizations have expounded on its impact. Rupert Murdoch, for instance, stated: "The Internet has been the most fundamental change during my lifetime and for hundreds of years. Someone the other day said, 'It's the biggest thing since Gutenberg,' and then someone else said 'No, it's the biggest thing since the invention of writing.'"[45]

In opposition, a few scholars have reminded us that technology-centered interpretations of the history of journalism do not capture what is most significant about the craft. In 2000, Carey wrote: "We have histories of the technology of journalism, of the media of journalism, of the great men, and now great women, who have shaped and dominated journalism, of the Supreme Court decisions that have defined and protected journalism; we have histories, in short, of everything about journalism except journalism itself."[46] Not all historians would agree that Carey's assessment of the state of journalism history still holds true, but today's loud discourse of revolutionary technological change makes this an opportune time to reflect on the status new technologies have been endowed with and the dynamics that have led to changes in news. For historians and nonhistorians alike, it is fruitful to consider the different perspectives one could take in regard to the impact of technology on news and society more generally. Anyone who believes technology is the prime shaper of the newspaper or other news products has adopted the ideology of the technological determinist. Those most rigid in this belief fall under the category of "hard determinism," which assumes that as technologies emerge, they create a future that cannot be avoided. Journalism historians influenced by this approach write of the "rise" and "spread" of the printing press, telegraph, radio, and television and rarely discuss contextual factors beyond governmental censorship in their interpretations of the history of news. They assume that such technologies are impossible for journalists, along with everyone else, to master.

On the opposite end of the spectrum are those who argue that changes in news take place not as a result of technologies but because of social, cultural, economic, and political conditions. Journalism historians who adopt this approach assume technological innovation related to the field of communication has been precipitated largely by social needs and trends. In the middle are those who assume that no technology or society alone explains history but that change occurs when technologies interact with sets of conditions present in a particular period of time. Brian Winston compared all of these positions in an essay titled "How Are Media Born?" He started with a pair of questions related to the power of technology that, he argued, run through many discussions of mass media: (1) how does technological change occur in mass communication? and (2) what effect, if any, does the technology have on the content—the output—of mass communication?[47]

Regardless of one's position on such questions, an understanding of the effects of technologies on news is enhanced if people's changing perceptions of time and space are considered. The essence of news is that it will not have impact unless it is fresh and timely, and today, individuals expect news to be instantaneously relayed across the globe. Before the telegraph, in contrast, people did not expect news to travel quickly, especially across great expanses of territory. But as journalists adopted this device in their gathering and distribution of news, expectations changed. And when coupled with events and contextual conditions such as wars or social conflict, the public's appetite for speedy and far-ranging news was whetted even more.

Beyond this, it is useful to break journalism into its four constituent elements, each of which may (or may not) be affected by emerging technologies: news gathering, as, for instance, via conversation, letter, rowboat, pigeon, telegraph, or telephone; news preparation, which has involved tools such as the pen, typewriter, and computer; news content, including a variety of evolving news forms and topics; and news dissemination, which has involved delivery of news via print, visual, broadcasting, and various other technologies that have affected the speed with which it is delivered, among other things.

Another point to consider is that exploring the historical antecedents of the technologies of journalism clarifies who and what the "true inventors" of those technologies have been. The individuals most closely associated with the invention of many of journalism's technologies did not create them for journalistic purposes.

Gutenberg, for example, did not invent the printing press with the newspaper in mind, and Guglielmo Marconi created radio for point-to-point communication rather than for broadcasting news. Eventually, experts and amateurs with fresh ideas about how to use such technologies for journalistic purposes came along, and the public also played a significant role in the transformation of the printing press and radio into technologies of reporting.

Factors outside human agency must also be considered by those seeking to understand the dynamics inherent in any changes the news undergoes. Such factors have included social conditions, re-form movements, and controversies; cultural values that influence and otherwise affect us in ways we are not always aware of; poli-tics and governmental systems, such as those directed by autocratic versus democratic ideologies; economic forces, including compe-tition, prosperity, and panic or depression; and unexpected events, such as hurricanes and earthquakes, that have made a difference in the history of news.

Technological innovation can lead to unanticipated results. As new technologies are adopted, old ones are at times abandoned. In addition, new technologies can lead to jurisdictional crises in work systems that cause some news workers to lose their occupational roles after new ones replace them. That said, once technologies have been successfully adopted, industry leaders have sometimes been averse to replacing them.

The technologies of journalism also have an impact on the news and the reputations of newspeople because of their acquired status as cultural agents and popular icons. As technologies have been in-troduced and adopted for use in American journalism, widely cir-culating discourses have connected them to core cultural values and converted them from mere tools to powerful cultural agents of change. Throughout its history, the printing press came to represent more than a device whose purpose was simply to print news stories on sheets of paper. Eventually, its operators and Americans in general came to view it as a symbol of progress, modernity, and enlightenment. Understanding how the journalistic press came to represent such ideals is just as critical as evaluating whether it has always lived up to them.

TWO

◇

HISTORICAL ANTECEDENTS

Technological histories of journalism usually start with accounts of Johannes Gutenberg's mid-fifteenth-century invention of the printing press. But any device as complex as the printing press should not be thought of as a single invention created by a single inventor. More accurately, Gutenberg's printing machine was an aggregation and adaptation of technologies that had been in use for centuries, such as screw-type wine and olive presses and woodblock print type. Similarly, while the history of the telegraph generally starts with the machine patented by Samuel F. B. Morse, Morse's work was based on that of his predecessors who experimented with electricity, magnets, and the use of wire as a conductor.

Another caveat related to the development of technologies concerns the intentions of their "inventors": rarely have these technologies been designed with what would later become their more popular uses in mind. It would appear that the first wheel, for instance, was not made to help move a cart. Although its exact origin is unknown, historians claim the wheel's earliest manifestation appeared when humans realized a heavy object could be moved more easily if something round, such as a log, was placed under it and the object was rolled over it. After a period of trial and error, humans eventually attached an improved version of this device to a cart.[48]

Similar to the story of the wheel, neither the printing press nor many of today's other important journalistic technologies were invented specifically for the purpose of circulating news reports. Gutenberg and the others involved in the development of society's earliest mechanical printing presses in fifteenth-century Europe were not thinking of producing newspapers as the purpose of their project. And though the inventors of the telegraph, the photograph, and the rest of journalism's technologies obviously had communication in mind during the first public demonstrations of their devices, the notion of appropriating them as crucial tools in the field had not yet been conceived.

A final cautionary note to consider when studying the histories of technologies relates specifically to their roles in the communication process. Simply put, the conveyance of news has never been totally dependent on printing and the other technologies typically associated with journalism. History's earliest formal news-gathering and dissemination enterprises were powered by humans who delivered the news orally and through handwritten newsletters. Smoke, mirrors, flags, torches, horses, carrier pigeons, rowboats, ships, and a variety of other things have also been used to gather and disseminate the news.[49]

The history of the newspaper, society's first major news medium, is traceable as far back as 59 B.C., when Rome's Julius Caesar required the posting of *Acta Diurna* (Daily Events) in prominent places across the provinces. The *Acta Diurna* carried information about military campaigns and plebiscite results, as well as news of gladiatorial contests, trials, executions, and notable births, deaths, and marriages. The Chinese also devised a system for spreading handwritten news—the *tipao*—that they used during the Han (202 B.C. to A.D. 221) and Tang (618–906) dynasties. Even after the emergence of the printing press, handwritten sheets have at times been essential sources of news. In Venice, handwritten news sheets called gazettes, containing information on wars and politics, were distributed in the mid-1500s. And as people moved west and south in early America's frontier days, people exchanged news in letters and handwritten newspapers before the first printing presses arrived.[50]

That said, accounts of the inventions and earliest uses of the technologies that eventually became intertwined with the production of news—the printing press, telegraph, photograph, motion picture, radio, television, computer, and Internet—provide a rich context for further discussion of the dynamics of change in the world of journalism. In addition to precipitating growth in the amount of news produced across the world, these technologies have been part of a complex mix of conditions affecting the speed with which news is delivered, how and why certain new forms of journalism have developed, and how and why certain extant forms of news have changed and others have disappeared from use.

In mid-fifteenth-century Europe, tools and techniques in use for hundreds of years came together to form the first mechanical printing press in the Western world. Centuries before, the Chinese and Koreans had been printing from negative relief, but not until early in the 1400s did this technique of printing with wooden blocks appear in Europe.[51] The person most often given credit for the invention of the printing press, although he did not work alone, was Johannes Gutenberg of Mainz (present-day Germany). In 1438, cloaked by a mantle of secrecy, Gutenberg entered into a partnership that culminated in the unveiling of a crude printing press, metal movable type, paper, and ink. In 1452, he entered into a business relationship with Johann Fust, a wealthy burgher. Throughout these years, Gutenberg experienced so many financial difficulties that he eventually lost his printing press and type to his debtors. Eventually, he was able to secure financial assistance that enabled him to build a new printing outfit. Little else is known about the remaining years of his life, including the exact date of his death in late 1467 or early 1468.[52]

The earliest products of Gutenberg's press included a poem, astrological and medical calendars, and a papal bull between 1448 and 1460. But by far the most famous product of that press was his forty-two-line Bible, a document published in 1455 that essentially started the mass production of books in the West. The printing press spread through continental Europe and eventually to England relatively quickly. By 1480, Venice had at least fifty printers, and by 1500, thousands of enterprising individuals had established printing presses across mainland Europe and England.[53]

Scholars have written that the printing press was one of the factors that helped spark a series of societal revolutions. Historian Elisabeth L. Eisenstein explored the relationship between the emergence of print culture in the West and the growth of a "reading public."[54] Among the effects of this development were the eventual displacement of the pulpit by the press and a weakening of local community ties. Looking more specifically at historical developments, the rise of modern science and the disruption of Western Christendom by the Protestant Reformation have often been attributed to the printing press.

What difference did the printing press make in the spread of news? Newspapers were not among the earliest products of Gutenberg's press, although broadsides that carried news flourished immediately at the dawn of printing. Single sheets of paper printed on only one side, broadsides were produced quickly and in large numbers, sometimes for a nominal fee, for distribution in town squares, taverns, and churches. News topics covered in the era's broadsides included current events, official proclamations and government decisions, public meetings and entertainment events, advocacy of political and social causes, products and services, and popular literary and musical efforts. In addition, the new presses began to publish newsbooks (pamphlets) that related events of common interest. The most popular broadsides and chapbook pamphlets featured stories of heroic feats, scandals, and amazing occurrences.[55] In 1470, a printed account of a tournament was circulated in Italy. In 1493, Christopher Columbus wrote a letter describing his discoveries in the New World that was reproduced in printed form.[56] In 1520, a newsbook, printed in England by Richard Fawkes, provided a four-page eyewitness description of the 1513 battle of Flodden Field. Authors and printers escaped arrest and other penalties by remaining anonymous or keeping a low profile, since it generally took a long time for these publications to come to the attention of authorities.

In the early years of the seventeenth century, operators of printing presses started publishing the double-sided news sheets that eventually came to be called newspapers. What is considered to be the earliest European newspaper, *Relation,* was published in 1609 in Strasbourg. Within the next forty years, despite governmental censorship, public demand led to the establishment of newspapers across continental Europe and England. Although small and crudely printed by later standards, papers would be published in Switzerland in 1610, the Hapsburg domains in central Europe in 1620, England in 1621, France in 1631, Denmark in 1634, Italy in 1636, Sweden in 1645, and Poland in 1661.[57]

Printing presses first arrived in the New World of the Americas in 1539 when an Italian printer, Juan Pablos, established a shop in Mexico City. Pablos, who went to Mexico as the agent of Seville printer Juan Cromberger, carried with him a press, Gothic types, paper, and materials for ink making. In 1550, he sent for Antonio de Espinosa, a type founder and die cutter who became his most notable successor in the printing business in Mexico, where he was active from 1559 to 1575. By 1600, nine presses were in operation in Mexico. Before and after the arrival of these presses, news circulated in Spanish America in the form of handwritten logbooks, accounts, and letters that were meant to keep the European imperial authorities informed about actions and key events that took place there. What is considered Mexico's first newspaper, *Gaceta de México,* was started in 1667 in Mexico City.[58]

In 1638, English colonists carried their first press to Cambridge (now Boston) in Massachusetts Bay Colony, but several decades would pass before more print shops were set up outside Boston. The first of these was established in Philadelphia in 1686; the colony of New York's first printing press was set up in the fledgling town of the same name in 1693; and in 1709, a press was established at Hartford, Connecticut. From there, presses were slowly established in the colonies' other developing towns and cities.[59]

In 1690, fifty-two years after the arrival of the Cambridge press, a newspaper was published for the first time in colonial America. Titled *Publick Occurrences, Both Forreign and Domestick,* the paper was issued by a rabble-rousing Englishman named Benjamin Harris.[60] Since he was not himself a printer, he hired a local craftsman by the name of Richard Pierce to get the paper out. Up to that point, early Americans received news largely through oral sources, locally printed single-sheeted news broadsides, handwritten newsletters, and imported printed newspapers. The lack of locally printed papers was probably not of great concern to the colonists, who were busy simply surviving in their first century of residence in primitive and isolated homes along the continent's eastern seaboard.

Harris had only lately arrived in America after being forced to flee his homeland to escape a jail term for seditious libel. He printed a notice in the paper stating that he would publish it at least once each month "or if any Glut of Occurrences happen, oftener." The paper was small: it filled about three-quarters of two six-by-ten-inch sheets of paper. Harris had not asked the authorities for permission to print his newspaper, a fact that caused him trouble immediately after he distributed it. Particularly irksome to the powers-that-be were Harris's accounts of the immoralities of the king of France and events related to the French and Indian War. He denounced the barbarous ways in which the Indian allies of the English had treated their French captives. Declaring "high Resentment and Disallowance of said Pamphlet," the government ordered that *Publick Occurrences* be "Suppressed and called in."[61] It was further ordered that nothing would be set to print in the future without prior authority. Harris's *Occurrences* thus became one of America's most important but short-lived papers.

Fourteen years later, in 1704, John Campbell started America's first regularly published paper, the *Boston News-Letter*.[62] Campbell was more successful than Harris because, as Boston's postmaster, he could publish his paper with authority as long as it did not contain anything objectionable. It never did. The *News-Letter*'s first issue, dated April 17–24, was a small sheet printed on both sides. It was full of news from England, including lengthy abstracts from mid-December issues of the *London Flying Post* and *London Gazette*. These articles concerned the papist (that is, French) threats to Scotland, Ireland, and England and warned of the "bloody designs of

Papists and Jacobites." An excerpt originally published on November 27, in Dublin, told of Irish "beginning to form themselves into bodies, and to plunder the Protestants of their arms and money." An extract of Queen Anne's speech to Parliament acquainted them with "unquestionable informations [*sic*] of very ill practices and designs carried on in Scotland by emissaries from France."[63]

The *News-Letter*'s attention to local occurrences was minimal. Occupying only one column on page two, its local news consisted of brief notices of maritime arrivals and activities, the appointment of Nathanael Byfield as judge of the Admiralty, and the preaching of an "excellent" sermon by Rev. Mr. Ebenezer Pemberton of Boston's Old South Church on 1 Thessalonians 4:11: "And do your own business." The *News-Letter* came out weekly, under several different publishers, until 1776.

Campbell's position as Boston's postmaster started a tradition in American journalism that tied the news closely to the U.S. Post Office. Anyone operating a postal office was ideally situated to receive news, copy it, and send it once it was inserted into a newspaper. According to press historian Richard Kielbowicz: "Public policy linked these complementary agencies of communication; inducements offered by the federal government made it attractive for private information processors—the press—to gather nonlocal news, while a public enterprise, the post office, moved the information across space. Far more than other government policies or actions touching the press, the routine operations of the post office shaped publications' contents, formats, and circulation."[64]

It would be more than a century before news became appreciably influenced by the wishes of advertisers. Campbell's first paper carried only one advertisement, an item he inserted himself: "This *News-Letter* is to be continued Weekly, and all persons who have any lands, houses, tenements, farms, ships, vessels, goods, wares or merchandise to be sold or let; or servants runaway, or goods Stoll [*sic*], or lost, may have the same inserted at a reasonable rate."[65]

Campbell's newspaper was the only one published in colonial America until December 21, 1719, when Boston's new postmaster, William Brooker, started the *Boston Gazette.* Having usurped Campbell's position, Brooker thought he should be allowed to publish his new paper under the old *News-Letter*'s imprimatur. When Campbell refused to give up his paper to Brooker, an animosity developed between the two men. Not long after Brooker began issuing the *Gazette,* Campbell wrote: "I pity the reader of the new paper; it is not fit reading for the people."[66]

On December 22, 1719, the day after Brooker started the *Gazette,* Andrew Bradford started a paper in Philadelphia, the first to be published outside Boston. The earliest issues of Bradford's paper, the *American Weekly Mercury,* consisted largely of news from London and continental Europe. In time, however, Bradford began publishing more local news, although he did get in a bit of trouble for doing so on at least one occasion. Newspapers were started in other colonies, such as New York, Maryland, and South Carolina, within the next several decades, but most towns went without papers. At the beginning of the American Revolution, only about thirty-seven newspapers were being published in the colonies.[67]

During the Revolution, the printing press played such a critical role in disseminating news and propaganda to proponents of both sides that its reputation and that of its operators and the newspapers they produced were irrevocably changed. Reflecting on the changes brought by the eighteenth century, Rev. Dr. Samuel Miller wrote:

It is worthy of remark that newspapers have almost entirely
changed their form and character within the period under review. For a long time after they were first adopted as a medium
of communication to the public, they were confined, in general,
to the mere statement of facts. But they have gradually assumed
an office more extensive, and risen to a more important station
in society. They have become vehicles of discussion, in which
the principles of government, the interests of nations, the spirit
and tendency of public measures, and the public and private characters of individuals, are all arraigned, tried, and decided. Instead,
therefore, of being considered now, as they once were, of small
moment in society, they have become immense moral and political engines, closely connected with the welfare of the state, and
deeply involved both its peace and prosperity.[68]

In the next several decades, Americans developed an infatuation
with the newspaper that was noticed by visitors from countries
that had not had a similar experience. In 1836, Alexis de Tocqueville wrote about this situation in *Democracy in America,* which he
compiled after a lengthy visit to the United States in 1831.[69] In a
discussion of Americans' love of associations and the role of newspapers in their everyday life, he remarked: "I am far from denying
that newspapers in democratic countries lead citizens to do very
ill-considered things in common; but without newspapers there
would be hardly any common action at all. So they mend many
more ills than they cause." About the producers of newspapers, de
Tocqueville observed: "They certainly are not great writers, but
they speak their country's language and they make themselves
heard."[70]

Americans' growing attachment to the newspaper was reflected in the burgeoning numbers and circulations of papers in

the nineteenth century. From 1800 to 1830, the number of newspapers grew from about 200 to more than 1,000, and after establishing America's first penny papers in the 1830s, news publishers in the country's urban centers experienced demands for newspapers that outstripped their ability to print them. Fueling this trend was an increase in the number of people who could afford to buy the newspapers that were sold for a penny rather than five or six cents. In addition, such people were fascinated by the local and crime-oriented news that publishers were starting to carry in their papers. By the end of the nineteenth century, more than 10,000 newspapers were printed across the United States, and the circulations of many grew to new heights. In 1897, the Sunday circulation of the *New York World* was estimated to be 568,000 copies.[71]

While population growth and other social, economic, and cultural developments sparked this phenomenal expansion in the number and circulation of newspapers, such expansion would not have been possible without improvements to Gutenberg's press. At the conclusion of the eighteenth century, most printers were still hand operating presses made of wood, and at best, such presses could produce no more than 240 copies per hour. But with the Industrial Revolution came a series of improvements that led to spectacular enhancement in the printing press's production capacity. Within decades, conversion to presses operated by steam made it possible to print thousands of sheets per hour.

One of the earliest improvements made to Gutenberg's press was the replacement of its wood with iron. The first iron printing press was built in England in about 1800 by Lord Earl Stanhope; the second was built in Philadelphia in 1813 by George Clymer. Stanhope's press was austere in appearance, whereas Clymer's Columbian presses were ornately decorated with sculpted figures such as the eagle and the caduceus. These and the many other iron presses manufactured during the early decades of the century enabled printers to work with larger sheets of paper. But since they were operated by hand, they were still slow.[72]

Not until steam was harnessed for printing would it be possible to greatly increase the speed of printing operations. Steam was introduced to the world of journalism in England in 1814 by Friedrich Koenig, a native of Eislebin, in Saxony.[73] A printer and newspaper publisher, Koenig had begun looking for ways to use steam for printing in 1802. Experimentation with steam engines began in the seventeenth century, and in 1712, the first operational and practical industrial engine was invented. After considerable work on his new press, Koenig moved to England in 1806. The nation was a refuge for inventors unable to find support for their ventures at home. With some difficulty, he acquired a patent for his invention in 1810, and after a number of necessary improvements, it was ready to go. On the morning of November 30, 1814, the publishers of the *London Times* distributed the first newspaper printed on a steam-operated press. The paper contained this announcement: "Our Journal of this day presents to the Public the practical result of the greatest improvement connected with printing since the discovery of the art itself."

Koenig's press helped the *Times* beat its competitors in the dissemination of important news. In a December 3, 1814, statement about their recent reports on Parliament, the paper's editors stated: "The length of the debates on Thursday, the day when Parliament was adjourned, will have been observed; on such an occasion the operation of composing and printing the last page must commence among all the journals at the same moment; and starting from that moment, we, with our infinitely superior circulation, were enabled to throw off our whole impression many hours before the other respectable rival prints."

Just before the *Times* unveiled its new steam press, some of its pressmen threatened vengeance against it and its inventor. Fearful that the machine would replace them, they anxiously waited to see what would happen on the first night it was used to print the *Times.* At the completion of the run, management informed the pressmen that they would be arrested if they resorted to violence. As it turned out, no arrests were necessary, and Koenig's presses advanced into newspaper pressrooms with little further trouble.

Koenig returned to Germany in 1816 after he experienced difficulties retaining the rights to his later development of a steam-operated book-printing press. Once settled in Oberzell on the Main, near Würzburg, he teamed up with Andreas Bauer and established a factory for the manufacturing of his presses. After his death in 1833, his partner and family carried on his work at Oberzell.

By 1885, approximately three thousand Koenig presses had been sold to publishers across the globe. In addition, many inventors had made improvements on Koenig's original press. Evidence that U.S. newspaper publishers were eager to replace their hand-operated presses with those powered by steam was plentiful in the columns of their papers. In 1837, an editorial originally published in the *Boston Daily Advertiser* and reprinted in the *New-York Spectator* declared: "There is no piece of machinery, upon which a greater degree of mechanical talent has been bestowed, for the production of a succession of inventions and improvements attended with the most surprising success, than the [steam] printing press. A large number of [steam] power presses are now in operation, entirely different one from another, yet each seeming when viewed by itself almost perfect, and each performing work with an admirable degree of perfection, without any skill on the part of the operator, other than what is necessary to lay on the sheet of paper."[74]

The next great improvement to Gutenberg's printing press was the introduction of a rotary press. Whereas Gutenberg's press printed paper between two flat surfaces, this machine printed paper between a supporting cylinder and a cylinder containing the printing plates. Richard March Hoe's machine, often referred to as a perfecting press, enabled the process to move much more quickly than before.[75] One year after Hoe received a patent for the invention in 1846, the first of his cylinder presses was installed. It developed such a reputation for speed that it was sometimes called the Hoe lightning press.[76]

The New York City newspaper establishment held Richard Hoe in such high esteem that, just four years after the installation of the first of his presses, a dinner was announced in his honor. Unable to attend, editors at a Cleveland newspaper published this comment: "The invitation reached us on the 26th, and as Editors cannot yet travel by telegraph even in this fast age, we could only be present on the festive occasion in spirit.—About one hundred guests were present, consisting of Editors, publishers, inventors."[77]

The sponsor of the dinner honoring Hoe was the famous *New York Sun,* America's first penny newspaper. In a column published about Hoe and his invention, the *Sun*'s publisher wrote:

> These "Lightning Presses" . . . enabled us greatly to extend our operations . . . from an edition of thirty-five thousand when the late "Lightning Presses" were first put in operation, the daily demand for the *New York Sun* now requires the issue of over fifty thousand copies. . . . The sight which this huge machine presents

when in operation, baffles all description. The sheets flying in and out with lightning rapidity, the buzz of wheels, the click of springs, the jumping of arms, and the movement of hundreds of other parts, give it the appearance of instinctive life.[78]

Newspaper publishers out of reach of the latest improved presses complained that they were so far away from the East Coast. A San Francisco publisher wrote of this after a boiler in his press-room burst just as he was starting to print a new edition of his paper. After thanking an editor in nearby Alta, California, for helping him get his edition out, he noted: "If some enterprising men would get out from New York a press something like those used there, it would pay well to run it here. There is not a steam printing press this side of the Rocky Mountains that can strike off our inside in less than about two hours."[79]

In 1886, another improvement to the printing press once again led to faster printing and bigger editions of the newspaper. Unveiled in 1886, Otto Mergenthaler's Linotype made it possible to set type by machine rather than by hand. Hailed by publishers who sought to put Mergenthaler's machine into operation as soon as possible, the Linotype led to discord among printers who believed it would lead to layoffs. In Louisville, Kentucky, on January 12, 1888, all but three of the *Courier-Journal*'s union printers left their posts after refusing to work with the representative of the Mergenthal Linotype Company sent from New York to train them.

By 1891, Linotype machines had so streamlined the printing industry that the Franklin Institute of Philadelphia gave Mergenthaler its prestigious John Scott Legacy Medal and Premium. According to the institute's awards committee, the Linotype machine had far surpassed earlier printers in is "celerity and capacity for work."[80] Such praise for the Linotype was echoed across the country. The Linotype was called "the Wonder of the Age" in a glowing 1893 column published in the *Milwaukee Journal*. Its author wrote:

> The linotype is indeed the triumph of human invention, and when it is seen at work it looks as though it had the brains of the inventor embodied in it. . . . It is the most practical machine that has ever been constructed, for it allows one pair of hands to do in the limited time allowed for the preparation of a daily paper the amount of work which otherwise requires many. Speed and accuracy are the two things required in such work, and it possesses both. . . . With the improvements made in its type-setting department today, The Journal will be able to give its readers a better and more complete paper throughout than was possible under the old methods. Every publication day in the year the paper will be printed from the new type, thus giving an impression so clear and bright that the reader's eye need never tire; a boon indeed to those who have had experience with papers that use type which under the most favorable circumstances, is soon battered and indistinct.[81]

The success of Mergenthaler's typesetting machine led other inventors to create their own versions, and publishers set up demonstrations of all of them at their national conventions. Late in 1891, the American Newspaper Publishers Association (ANPA) announced it was sponsoring a typesetting machine contest at the *Chicago Evening Post*. A report on the contest, published in an Atchison, Kansas, newspaper, stated: "Newspaper proprietors and publishers in all parts of the country manifest great interest in this contest, the first of the kind ever held, and it is expected a large number of publishers will take advantage of the opportunity to see the various machines work together and make comparisons as to their relative merits." With a prophetic comment, the story concluded: "It is confidently believed that in the near future some of these wonderful typesetting machines will be developed to such an extent that the news of the world will be put in type direct from telegraph wires."[82]

While big-city newspapers installed typesetting machines as soon as they could, publishers in small towns would have to be patient because it would be some time before it was practical for them to do so. In 1893, the National Editorial Association's annual convention held a business session titled "Are Type-Setting Machines Practical for Dailies and Weeklies in Smaller Cities?" E. S. Slack, the Cheyenne, Wyoming, newspaper editor who conducted the program, said: "Without a doubt the type-setting machine, or linotype, has come to stay, and will eventually drive out hand composition in all the country villages. It will, however, call for a high class of skilled operators and machinists which it will take many years to create."[83]

News publishers began adding electricity to their technological toolboxes late in the nineteenth century. Electric motors, which had been in use since the early years of the Industrial Revolution, came relatively late to the field of news publishing. An article printed in a 1892 St. Paul, Minnesota, paper, under the title "Printing by Electricity," reported that the proprietors of the *Daily Gazette* in Birmingham, England, had recently used electricity to drive their printing machines. The author stated: "The Gazette is absolutely the first daily paper in the world that has been produced by that form of power, which bids fair to revolutionize the whole system of machines, and leave steam, and even gas far beyond as motive forces. . . . The smoke and heat of engine furnaces are done away with, and one great advantage is that the power is available by day and night, and the two machines, each capable of producing 20,000 copies of the *Gazette,* ready folded, per hour, can be set in motion at any moment."[84]

The *Gazette*'s electrically powered press was based on the work of Vermont native Thomas Davenport, who invented the world's first rotating electrical motor in 1834.[85] A self-educated blacksmith, Davenport was awarded a government patent for his motor in 1837. Not long after, he began publishing *The Magnet,* the first technical journal dedicated to the study of electricity. The author of an *American Journal of Science and Arts* article on Davenport's achievements concluded: "Science has thus, most unexpectedly, placed in our hands a new power, of great, but unknown energy."[86] Davenport set up a laboratory and workshop near Wall Street in hopes of attracting investors, and to further advertise his motor, he harnessed it to his printing press to turn out a publication titled *The Electro-magnet and Mechanics Intelligencer.*[87]

During the twentieth century, inventors made countless additional improvements to the printing press. But preceding such developments were the introductions of two additional categories of inventions that affected the news, along with the basic work tasks of those who practiced journalism: visual and telecommunication technologies. The latter, starting with the telegraph in the 1840s, enabled individuals to communicate across great expanses of space more quickly and efficiently than was previously possible. Eventually, telecommunications allowed journalists to return to one of humanity's oldest news forms—that which was dependent on the spoken word rather than print. And the former, beginning with the simplest woodcut images but culminating in the development of the field of photojournalism, helped transform journalism into a product in which words combined with images conveyed the news.

Woodcuts were in use even before the advent of the printing press, whereas engraving and lithography were eighteenth- and early-nineteenth-century visual innovations. By the middle of the nineteenth century, illustrated newspapers that reproduced pictorial representations of the news began to grow in popularity in the United States. Two decades earlier, in the late 1830s, the earliest photographic technology—the daguerreotype—was announced in France. And after the daguerreotype quickly jumped the Atlantic to America, many other types of photographs were invented. Not until 1880, however, would it be possible to insert a photographic image into a newspaper. The halftone process was the invention that made this possible, and by early in the twentieth century, photojournalism had become a major element of newspaper and magazine reporting. In time, individuals involved in experimentation with photographic equipment developed the handheld camera and photographic film that made it possible to take and develop pictures much more efficiently. An equally important factor affecting the development of the field of photojournalism was the public's gradual appreciation for photographic representations of people and situations that were previously considered private. In addition, the growth of photo agencies designed to forward the interests of those involved in the new field of photojournalism would further impact the ways photographs were used within the news.[88]

Today's magazines are among journalism's heaviest users of photographs, but not until long after they originally appeared on the American scene in 1741 would magazines become visually oriented. As with the newspaper, the growth of the magazine in early America was extremely slow because conditions and technologies at the time did not favor their development. In fact, it would be nearly two centuries before magazines published solely to relate the news were started, and the photograph would be part of these developments. In 1923, Henry Luce and Briton Hadden announced the establishment of America's first "newsmagazine," *Time,* which was slated to emphasize national and international news. Thirteen years later, Luce started *Life* magazine, a photo-journalistic weekly that covered a wide range of topics. In his magazine's slogan, Luce said he wanted his readers "to see life; to see the world; to witness great events; to watch the faces of the poor and the gestures of the proud; to see strange things." *Life*'s popularity with readers declined as television increasingly grabbed their attention in the 1950s and 1960s.[89]

The public's favorable response to *Time* encouraged others to start newsmagazines. One of the first was *Newsweek,* which was established on February 17, 1933, by Thomas J. C. Martyn, a former *Time* magazine foreign editor. The public would see the introduction of another weekly newsmagazine in 1933 when David Lawrence started *U.S. News* to cover national news. Notable for its thorough coverage of prominent news events in Washington, D.C., it also often carried the complete texts of major speeches and documents coming out of the nation's capital. In 1945, Lawrence established *World Report* to treat international news, and in 1948, he merged the two under the title *U.S. News and World Report.*

Another visual technology eventually used in the communication of news stories was the motion picture. In the 1890s, experimentation with film culminated in its earliest public displays. After 1895, short films depicting sports and political events were regularly shown in America's fledgling community of motion picture theaters. In 1911, the Pathé Company in France began to use motion pictures for the first time for the distribution of news. The earliest films—called newsreels—were "actualités," that is, depictions of true-life events filmed outdoors by the earliest cameras. By World War I, newsreels were a staple along with the main featured film. In the sound era after 1926, five newsreel companies predominated: Fox Movietone, Paramount, Universal, Warner-Pathé (owned by Radio-Keith-Orpheum [RKO] after 1931), and Hearst Metrotone. Each month, a newsreel titled *March of Time,* a program that resembled a newsmagazine, was released in theaters across America. Among the most famous of America's newsreel stories was that of the Hindenberg explosion on May 6, 1937. All the newsreel companies had photographers at Manchester, New Jersey, where the incident occurred at the Lakehurst Naval Air Station, and the National Broadcasting Company (NBC) sent recording devices to gather sound.[90]

The popularity of the newsreels was to be eclipsed by the growing popularity of television in the 1950s. Queen Elizabeth II's 1953 coronation gave the newsreels one of their "last moments of glory."[91] While television news abruptly ended the era of the newsreels, they should be credited with the impact they had on the news agendas of American moviegoers. During the 1930s and 1940s, a time often referred to by historians as the golden era of the movies, some people went to their neighborhood theaters a number of times each week. News was also distributed in newspapers and on the radio, but the newsreels' moving pictures added a fascinating visual dimension to journalism.

Like these visual technologies, telecommunications also began to impact journalism in the nineteenth century. As in the case of the printing press, the man who most often is given credit for the invention of the earliest telegraphy machine, Samuel F. B. Morse, did not create it with the intention of using it to send news. Morse's invention was first demonstrated in 1844 through the exchange of messages over a line strung from Baltimore, Maryland, to Washington, D.C. Within two years, a group of five enterprising New York newspaper publishers began talking about using the telegraph for the collection and distribution of news.[92]

In the 1870s, experimentation involving the transmission of wireless radio waves began, and in 1898, Guglielmo Marconi opened the world's first "wireless" factory in England. Starting in 1898, Marconi's newly founded wireless company began sending the Dublin Daily Express minute-by-minute coverage of sporting events such as the Kingstown Regatta American Cup races. The wireless eventually led to the broadcasting of messages to large audiences rather than individual radio operators. Around 1915, radio enthusiasts such as David Sarnoff began posing the idea that the new medium could be used for broadcasting, that is, the dissemination of messages to wide audiences. In August 1920, station WWJ in Detroit was the first to provide regular radio programming, and in November that same year, KDKA went on the air in Pittsburgh. In 1924, a radio hookup broadcast the Democratic and Republican national conventions. The inaugural address of that year's presidential winner, Calvin Coolidge, was broadcast to twenty-four stations. In 1925, radio newscasters covered the year's major trial, the Scopes monkey trial, which took place in Dayton, Tennessee. In 1930, Lowell Thomas began America's first regularly broadcast radio news program.[93]

The technological origins of television—which is essentially an extension of radio—lie in the nineteenth century, when experimentation with the fundamental technologies that would eventually be combined to create television began. Just as Morse's telegraph demonstrated that messages could be transmitted through wires, another nineteenth-century scientist's work helped lay the foundation for the technology of television. English physicist Alexander Bain's 1842 facsimile device enabled him to transmit characters and words over wire. Later, German scientist Paul Nipkow invented a perforated, spiral-distributing disk that would become the first successful method for scanning moving images, and in 1900, Russian Constantin Perskyi made the first known use of the word *television* at the World's Fair in Paris. In 1906, Lee de Forest created the Audion vacuum tube, the first device with the ability to amplify signals. In 1907, Campbell Swinton and Boris Rosing suggested cathode tubes could be used to transmit images. Independent of each other, they developed scanning methods capable of reproducing images.[94]

Using these and other developments as a basis, scientists were poised on the brink of inventing television by the 1920s. Research was proceeding along two paths: some scientists were involved in the development of television as a mechanical process, and others were exploring television as an electronic device. American Charles Jenkins and Scotsman John Baird followed the mechanical model, while Philo Farnsworth, working independently in San Francisco, and Russian émigré Vladimir Zworykin, working for Westinghouse and later the Radio Corporation of America (RCA), advanced the electronic model. In 1923, Zworykin invented the iconoscope, a tube for use in television's first cameras, and in 1929 the cathode-ray tube, also known as the kinescope, which essentially was the first modern television picture tube.

On April 9, 1927, Bell Telephone and the U.S. Department of Commerce demonstrated the first long-distance use of TV, between Washington, D.C., and New York City. Secretary of Commerce Herbert Hoover remarked: "Today we have, in a sense, the transmission of sight for the first time in the world's history. Human genius has now destroyed the impediment of distance in a new respect, and in a manner hitherto unknown."[95] Also that year, Philo Farnsworth filed for a patent on the first complete electronic television system, which he called the Image Dissector.

In 1928, the Federal Radio Commission issued the first license for a television station, W3XK, to Charles Jenkins, an inventor from Dayton, Ohio, who had promoted the concept of mechanical television since the late nineteenth century. In 1930, Jenkins aired television's first commercial. In 1933, Iowa State University (station W9XK) started broadcasting twice-weekly television programs in cooperation with radio station WSUI. By 1936, about two hundred television sets were in use worldwide. That same year, an important step was taken when American Telephone & Telegraph (AT&T) laid the first coaxial cable lines, between New York and Philadelphia. These cables are still used to transmit television, telephone, and data signals.[96]

In 1939, Vladimir Zworykin and RCA conducted experimental broadcasts from the Empire State Building. Television was demonstrated at the New York World's Fair and the San Francisco Golden Gate International Exposition. RCA's David Sarnoff used his company's exhibit at the 1939 World's Fair as a showcase for the first presidential speech on television and to introduce RCA's new line of television receivers—some of which had to be coupled with a radio if one wanted to hear sound. Also that year, the Dumont Company started manufacturing television sets.

By the late 1940s, those who had invested in television during the previous several decades hoped they were at the beginning of a new era, and they would not be disappointed. As growing numbers of people took televisions home during the 1950s, the period became known as the decade of television. Television's first regular news broadcast, *CBS TV News,* began in 1948 and was hosted by Douglas Edwards. Edward R. Murrow started his famous *See It Now* show in 1951. Two years later, he launched *Person to Person,* and for the next six years, he took his viewers on weekly trips to the homes of famous people. In 1963, it appeared that television had surpassed newspapers and magazines as an information source when a Roper Poll indicated 36 percent of Americans found television to be a more reliable source for news, compared to 24 percent who favored print.[97]

Print journalists' earliest forays into the computing world involved the gradual replacement of their old typewriters by two technologies: the optical character reader and the video display terminal (VDT). The users of optical character readers worked with electronic typewriters to write copy that was then "read" and "set" in type. The video display terminal, which incorporated an electronic keyboard interfaced with a screen similar to a television set, allowed a journalist to have direct access to a computer that operated a typesetting machine. Concerns about the detrimental impact of these new technologies on news quality proved unfounded. In a survey conducted in the mid-1980s, newspaper journalists reported that the VDT enabled them to better handle late-breaking stories, gave them a stronger sense of ownership over their work, and in general led to better newspapers.

In television news production facilities, computerized systems that linked together personnel using video display terminals were first adopted in the early 1980s. Manufactured by NewStar, television's earliest newsroom computer programs allowed reporters to write scripts and read wire stories. Later software enabled news producers to organize newscasts and create detailed rundowns of the news program's content. Newsroom computer automation systems were developed to simplify the technical and operational parts of compiling a television news program, improve communication within the news operation, and replace human machine operators where possible. In a discussion of the advantages of having a computerized newsroom during the 1991 Gulf War, an NBC journalist said: "Computers allow you to get information to and from people better. Hundreds of people can see it. We put the scripts of news on the computer—the rundown for the nightly news."[98]

Television news producers started to use computer-based graphics and video-editing systems in the early 1990s, although their price tag would slow their spread. Early nonlinear video-editing equipment was just as expensive, but newer programs such as Apple Final Cut Pro and Adobe Premiere have become more affordable. Nonlinear video editing is replacing traditional tape-to-tape editing, and some stations have established all-digital workflow. Overall, such technologies have streamlined news gathering and production, enabling television producers to provide their audiences with more on-the-scene and up-to-date news coverage.

Before the mid-1980s, anyone interested in establishing a weekly or daily newspaper was required to purchase an office full of publishing equipment worth hundreds of thousands of dollars. But the cost of starting a new periodical dropped greatly in 1985 when a trio of new technologies—the Apple Macintosh computer, the Hewlett-Packard Laserjet printer, and Aldus Page-Maker—became available. Thus was born the field of desktop publishing (DTP), a development that many have said led to a revolution. The term *desktop publishing* is often attributed to Paul Brainerd, who developed the PageMaker program in the early 1980s. A 1986 report on desktop publishing defined DTP as "preparation of typeset or near typeset documents on desktop computers (personal computers). All text composition, page makeup, manipulation of digitized graphics and integration of text and graphics are performed on desktop computers."[99]

In addition to offering substantial savings in production costs, desktop publishing caught on because it gave authors far greater access to the entire production process. The time involved in sending copy and proofs back and forth from printer to author, for example, was shortened. Among the most popular products generated by desktop publishers was the newsletter. A few of these "new" DTP journalists who used their "presses" for noble purposes became famous. In 1991, when Communist hard-liners deposed Soviet president Mikhail Gorbachev, they also closed the major news media. Refusing to kowtow to the leaders of the putsch, a graphic designer with a desktop publishing setup typed, printed, and distributed several objections to the coup and its imposition of censorship. Observers of the incident claim these actions contributed to the revolt's demise.

In the 1980s, a few news organizations began experimenting with innovative electronic technologies in hopes of developing less expensive alternatives to print delivery systems. Among these projects were teletext, videotex, audiotex, bulletin board systems (BBS), and fax news. After all of these journalistic ventures were abandoned because they failed to generate revenue, the attention of news publishers turned to the World Wide Web. As it emerged in the waning years of the twentieth century, the Internet's Web began to attract so much attention that by 1994, it had edged out telnet to become the Net's second most popular offering. In the process, it attracted the attention of a group known today as cyber-journalists. The relatively low cost of publishing news on the World Wide Web has been a major factor in the emergence of cyberjournalism. Another advantage of the Web is that it exists outside the boundaries of traditional journalism. Together, these conditions precipitated the establishment of new Web-based journalistic voices characterized by strong personalities and editorial viewpoints.

One of the best known of these news sites is the Drudge Report, a controversial news source that comments on politics and other media. Rather than mimicking traditional journalism, its creator, Matt Drudge, reprints materials gleaned from a variety of sources, not all of which are reputable. Drudge has a proclivity for using anonymous sources in high places, and he is notorious for considering stories publishable once he is 80 percent certain of their veracity. He has made a number of enemies in the mainstream press, as well as among those covered in his reports; for instance, Drudge became a codefendant in a $30 million lawsuit filed against him and America Online (AOL) by White House aide Sidney Blumenthal. One of his talents is his ability to scoop mainstream media on many occasions. The Drudge Report was the first to break the Bill Clinton/Monica Lewinsky story, as well as the news that California voters had recalled Governor Gray Davis and that Arnold Schwarzenegger was going to win the gubernatorial race by a landslide.

In 1998, another journalistic Web site was launched under the title Tabloid Column. Its owners promised the new site would be a "daily news service for readers weary of boring journalism."[100] Set up like a mainstream news service, its contents are anything but traditional. Its mission statement asserts that it "exists to shock and enlighten readers with the horrors, follies, frauds, heroes and villains of the real world—and to amuse and educate with true reports of bizarre people, weird events and odd science." To meet these goals, the editors offer visitors to the site irreverently written stories situated under loud, tabloid-style headlines.

Along with America's nontraditional journalists, well-established newspapers began to explore the Web's potential for news dissemination. One of the first papers to establish an online presence was the *News & Observer,* a regional daily published for citizens in the Raleigh-Durham area of North Carolina. In 1994, the paper established *Nando Times,* which it claims was one of the Web's first online newspapers. But unlike the *News & Observer,* most well-established papers have not been too anxious to rush into the world of the Internet.[101] Some of the earliest editors of online newspapers simply copied and pasted the contents of their already published papers into their digital editions. And though others have been more willing to experiment with the World Wide Web's capabilities, few have been ready to take advantage of all that it has to offer.

A quick look at today's hundreds of online editions of national, regional, and small-town newspapers would seem to indicate that mainstream journalism is flourishing on the Web. But the untrained eye misses what experts have seen in their research: traditional media, on the whole, have not been moving rapidly toward technological innovation, and most of the progress made in the growth of the Web as a news medium has resulted from the efforts of nontraditional journalists and nonnews organizations such as Google. Recent reports, however, suggest the situation is changing. The *Annual Report on the State of the News Media,* a publication compiled by the Project for Excellence in Journalism, identified one of the major trends of the year 2006: "Traditional media do appear to be moving toward technological innovation—finally."[102]

Short for *Weblogging,* the term *blogging* is used to describe a recent and fast-expanding form of Web-based writing and publishing that is making inroads into the world of journalism. The term *Weblog* was first used in 1997 on a site called Robot Wisdom (robotwisdom.com) that carried links to Web sites of interest to its publisher. Blogs are personal home pages that writers use to record their thoughts along with any information they find interesting in a chronological, diary-like, day-to-day format. Free downloadable software is available to anyone wanting to start a blog. The software has its origins at the National Center for Supercomputing Applications at the University of Illinois, where it was designed as a listing of updatable Web links to carry up-to-date news items about computing developments. Blogs are increasing exponentially in number. A report released early in 2006 counted over twenty-seven million Weblogs, a figure more than sixty times greater than that recorded just three years previously. Today's blogs cover a plethora of topics, and some provide their readers with news related to their primary areas of interest. Blogs also facilitate two-way communication, unprecedented in the traditional news environment.

In the past several years, the term *news aggregator* has entered the news business lexicon through the influence of software that retrieves syndicated Web content in the form of a Web feed. Operators of Internet search engines including Yahoo! and Google provide news aggregators among their products. *Google News* was first introduced to the public in April 2002, and today, Google publishes its aggregator in more than twenty languages. For its English-language users, the content of *Google News* draws from more than forty-five hundred news Web sites. The service includes articles published during the preceding thirty days on news Web sites. Users of *Google News* can search and sort the results by date and time of publication.

Podcasting is another online application that has recently attracted the attention of journalists. Precursors to podcasting existed prior to the Internet, but none were extremely successful. The word *podcast* was invented in 2004, by combining *iPod* and *broadcasting*. Podcasting makes it possible for people to collect programs from any number of different sources for listening or viewing whenever they please offline on their computers or through portable listening devices such as iPods or other digital audio players. This capability gives podcasters an advantage over broadcasters, who disseminate programming according to preset schedules.

Another thing that differentiates podcasting from earlier digital audio and video delivery systems is its use of syndication feed enclosures, a technology created for use with Really Simple Syndication (RSS) software. The idea was first proposed in an October 2000 report by Tristan Louis, an author, entrepreneur, and blogger, and was then picked up by Dave Winer, a software developer and an author of the RSS format. Winer demonstrated how an audio file could become an "enclosure" within a Weblog message by enclosing a Grateful Dead song in his *Scripting News* Weblog on January 11, 2001. Two years later, Winer created a special RSS-with-enclosures feed for Christopher Lydon's Weblog. Using Winer's special feed, Lydon was able to post twenty-five in-depth interviews with bloggers, futurists, and political figures on his blog. From October 2003 to early 2004, a series of meetings and other collaborations led to the coining of the term *podcasting*.

In September 2004, Carl Franklin, publisher of an audio talk show, started the first official podcast production company. As word spread, podcasting became especially popular among those interested in technology, music, and movies. The first national-level politician to hold his own podcast was North Carolina senator John Edwards, who started podcasting in March 2005. In November of that year, the Podcaster News Network was launched, its content largely focused on national and international news, sports, business, popular culture, politics, and religion. U.S. radio, television, and newspaper owners have responded with keen interest in podcasting, and a number of them have added it to their growing array of Web site offerings.

In addition to the printing press and the other major forms of technology that have come to play central roles in the delivery of news, other devices have been adopted by journalists and impacted the way in which they collect and process the news. The first known use of the telephone in the news process, for example, took place on February 17, 1877, when a *Boston Globe* reporter sent a dispatch that was published the next morning under the headline SENT BY TELEPHONE. The dispatch read: "This special dispatch of the *Globe* has been transmitted by telephone in the presence of 20 people, who have thus been witnesses to a feat never before attempted—the sending of news over the space of sixteen miles by the human voice."[103] Not until after the turn of the twentieth century would telephone transmissions be of sufficient quality to be used widely in the reporting process. In 1901, the first reports of the assassination of President William McKinley were relayed to points west by telephone.

Another machine that changed how journalists produced stories was the typewriter. Experimentation with early machines that made it possible to type words on paper started in America in the 1820s. Such devices attracted little attention until 1868, however, when Christopher Latham Shoales created a more practical machine that *Scientific American* magazine dubbed the typewriter. Initially, typewriters were used by literary figures and government employees. Mark Twain was an early typewriter enthusiast, and he invested money in its technical development. Typewriters finally started showing up at newspaper offices, according to one account, after word spread, in 1884, that telegraphers at the Nashville office of the Western Associated Press were using them. After hearing that editors were hailing the typewriter's cleaner, more legible copy, newspapers and telegraph operators all over the country adopted the machines.[104]

Technologies are typically defined as "tools" that help us perform tasks, but they can also be conceived of as "techniques" that can help people solve problems. Through periods of trial and error, experts in many fields have developed techniques that have benefited their professions as well as society more generally. In the medical field, the use of germs to inoculate people against disease serves as an example of a highly successful technique perfected over a long period of time. Similarly, throughout the history of journalism, techniques have been developed to improve the ability of news workers to provide the public with comprehensive and comprehensible journalistic reports. Examples include the formulation of systems that facilitate news delivery, the invention of the news beat and the interview process, the development of the summary lead, and the formulation of the inverted pyramid style of organizing news stories.

Historical accounts of the development of these techniques have been written, although their authors have not necessarily thought of them as "technologies of journalism." Scholars have documented the early growth of America's newspaper delivery system as a process related to the development of close ties between newspaper printers and the postal system. Press historians have traced the origins of the routines of news beats and interviewing back to the mid-1830s, when employees of the era's new penny papers increasingly left their offices to visit the courts and neighborhoods to gather crime-related news. And others seeking to understand the origins of the inverted pyramid news, that is, stories organized to begin with the most critical information, have explored the dynamics that led writers to prepare their stories in this way.

In addition to defining them as tools and techniques, society has also conceived of technologies as social and/or cultural forces with functions and effects that extend far beyond the purposes their creators imagined them serving. When technologies first emerge, they are often viewed with wonder. But as individuals and groups begin to appropriate them in pursuit of their own agendas, society's views of innovative technologies are subject to change. Gunpowder, for example, is a compound that was unconnected to the field of weaponry in its earliest manifestation.

Searching for a secret to immortality, the early Chinese began experimenting with the substance, and later, they would use it to treat skin diseases and kill insects. In roughly A.D. 850, the compound's formula was published in a book, along with the warning that "smoke and flames result." By early in the next millennium, the Chinese were producing millions of weapons that depended on this powder as a propellant. As the use of this chemical compound shifted from health to war, people's conceptions regarding its social and cultural power shifted from an appreciation of its healing abilities to a concern about its destructive potential.

Much like the compound that would come to be known as gunpowder, the technologies of journalism have tended to be seen as powerful symbols of either good or bad. In periods immediately following the emergence of new communication technologies, people have often responded with enthusiasm. But the uses journalists and others have sometimes made of the printing press and the field's other major technologies have led to criticism and even official censorship. In the late decades of the fifteenth century, commentary on the new printing presses revealed a great appreciation for their utility and potential impact. Aware that the inventions his generation was witnessing would be profoundly important in history, Marsilio Ficino (1433–1499) wrote of the printing press in a 1492 letter to one of his friends:

> If we are to call any age golden, it is beyond doubt that age which brings forth golden talents in different places. That such is true of this our age [no one] will hardly doubt. For this century, like a golden age, has restored to light the liberal arts, which were almost extinct: grammar, poetry, rhetoric, painting, sculpture, architecture, music . . . and all this in Florence. Achieving what had

been honored among the ancients, but almost forgotten since, the age has joined wisdom with eloquence, and prudence with the military art. . . . This century appears to have perfected astronomy, in Florence it has recalled the Platonic teaching from darkness into light . . . and in Germany . . . [there] have been invented the instruments for printing books.[105]

But leaders were quick to realize the printing press could lead to dissent, and by the time the additional presses arrived on the shores of North America, authorities in many countries had issued laws or edicts that controlled their use. When the town of Cambridge in Massachusetts Bay Colony became the home of America's first printing press in 1638, few but its operators and the small group who had access to its products regarded it with much appreciation. In 1662, the colony's general court appointed two individuals as licensers of the press, instructing them that no book should be published without permission. Although the British system of licensing began to crumble there early in the next century, authorities in other colonies imposed strict censorship. When Lord Effingham arrived as governor in Virginia Colony in 1683, for example, he brought with him instructions from the home ministry to forbid the use of printing presses. Not until 1729 would printing be allowed in the colony, and from that date until the Revolution, Virginia would have but one printing press. Up to the Revolution, the governors of all the colonies were permitted under royal decree to censor their subjects' use of the press whenever they felt the need to do so.

Respect for the press among early Americans grew over the eighteenth century, especially as it helped the American patriots throw out the British. While there were still those who derided the press and its operators, the printing press had served as an indispensable political tool in the hands of the patriots and also become valued for its ability to educate and enlighten. Such appreciation, along with fresh memories of British press censorship, culminated in the eventual inclusion of the press in the First Amendment to the U.S. Constitution. The power that the operators of the press wielded in the waning years of the century triggered a backlash in the form of the Alien and Sedition Acts of 1798. But after the laws were allowed to expire in Thomas Jefferson's administration, Americans in the early Republic exhibited much less taste for the idea of press censorship. In his 1803 retrospective on the 1700s, Rev. Dr. Samuel Miller wrote that the press and its newspapers "have become immense moral and political engines, closely connected with the welfare of the state, and deeply involving both its peace and prosperity."[106]

Like the printing press, television has been viewed by society as both a positive and a negative force. In reminiscing on his first exposure to television, British dramatist and screenwriter Dennis Potter (1935–1994) said: "I first saw television when I was in my late teens. It made my heart pound. Here was a medium of great power, of potentially wondrous delights, that could slice through all the tedious hierarchies of the printed word and help to emancipate us from many of the stifling tyrannies of class status and gutter-press ignorance. At a crucial period of my life it threw open the 'magic casement' on great sources of mind-scape."[107] Grace Murrell Nisbet (1900–1986), shortly after her appointment in 1948 as the first head of television news at the British Broadcasting Corporation (BBC), declared: "Television is a bomb about to burst."[108]

Within a few decades, such glowing reviews had all but disappeared, except among those in the television business. In contrast to his comment on television's "potentially wondrous delights,"

Potter remarked in a 1977 forum on television: "Never in the entire history of drama in all its forms has so much been produced for so large an audience with so little thought."[109] And in 1958, broadcast journalist Edward R. Murrow warned the owners of television: "This instrument can teach, it can illuminate, yes, it can even inspire. But it can do so only to the extent that humans are determined to use it to those ends. Otherwise, it is merely lights and wires in a box."[110]

As had happened in the era of the colonial press, licenses from the government were eventually required for the transmission of radio and television signals. In return for being granted a license, broadcasters must, according to the Federal Communications Commission (FCC), submit to periodic reviews of their efforts to ascertain and meet the needs of their communities.[111]

As required by this FCC order, commercial television news providers have offered the public journalistic reports on a wide range of topics. But sometimes, the values of television news professionals have clashed so violently with the standards of certain segments of their audiences that the field has been subject to intense criticism. Since the advent of television news programming, broadcasters have paid considerable attention to crime, and this has led to criticism. Among the worries of critics are that a heavy emphasis on crime news will lead to more crime and that heavy doses of crime news could cultivate a heightened sense of general fearfulness among television viewers.

Major studies designed to measure the effects of television and film violence were seen as early as the 1960s. In a 1978 study, George Gerbner found a correlation between the level of television viewing and a "mean world syndrome"—that is, the perception that most people are selfish and underhanded. Gerbner, who has been studying this phenomenon ever since, wrote in 1994:

The mean world syndrome results in a reduced sensitivity to the consequences of violence along with an increased sense of vulnerability and dependence—and therefore a demand for repression from the government. This has enormous political fallout. It's impossible to run an election campaign without advocating more jails, harsher punishment, more executions, all of the things that have never worked to reduce crime but have always worked to get votes. It's driven largely, although not exclusively, by television-cultivated insecurity.[112]

From the printing press to the podcast, historical accounts of the development and adoption of technologies for the gathering, processing, and dissemination of news have been told and retold in countless popular and scholarly formats. Although these stories are entertaining and provide meaningful information, they are just a starting point. A more nuanced understanding of how technologies such as the printing press and camera have affected the news and become thought of as cultural agents and symbols requires delving more deeply into the dynamics of change in the history of journalism.

THREE

THE DYNAMICS OF CHANGE

Although an appropriate starting point in any history of journalism, understanding the role of invention in the process of change requires a consideration of complex dynamics obscured by time. For one thing, technologies are more than tools and techniques designed by inventors to solve problems or advance humanity. They do not naturally "spread" or "flow" through society like some unstoppable force. Instead, they acquire meaning as people integrate them into their daily routines. Likewise, they are cultural constructions that become embodiments of society's values and traditions. And once people commonly use particular technologies for the completion of important tasks, unraveling how they became so important in the first place is even more difficult.

The technologies most often associated with journalism—the printing press, telegraph, camera, radio, television, computer, and Internet—were invented for purposes that had little to do with the news. But as printers and publishers began using them to disseminate news, they became associated with journalism. As mentioned earlier, Johannes Gutenberg was not thinking of journalism when he built the first printing press, but within a few decades, printers were using his invention to spread the news. Radio's earliest inventors considered the wireless to be a point-to-point communication tool, but after World War I, enthusiasts promoted radio as a broadcast medium. The developers of history's earliest cameras used them to take portraits, but by the Civil War, Mathew Brady and a few others were taking pictures for journalistic purposes. Despite the vision these individuals shared, societal and cultural conditions supportive of the idea that the camera should be used to record the news did not did not evolve until a few decades later.

Although a comparison of these stories reveals differences in details, the stories as a whole demonstrate that technologies will only be adopted for use in journalism if environmental conditions and human motivations interact in just the right ways. A society's state of development and economic health, level of government support for press freedom, and literacy rate all affect the adoption and continued viability of technologies for the dissemination of news. Events that can impact the technological dimensions of news delivery systems include wars, political unrest, and natural disasters such as famines, epidemics, earthquakes, and hurricanes. But just as societal and economic conditions and unexpected events can lead to an increased use of certain technologies for news, they can also lead to their abandonment by the media.

In the early Middle Ages, an individual's life was so intensely local in many places across the world that what took place outside the immediate community was not relevant, at least when compared to later cultures. Even after the Renaissance, a period when the world's new press operators had set up printing shops across continental Europe and England that were publishing newspapers, conditions remained so primitive that the adoption of technologies for news purposes had not yet developed into a priority. Such was certainly the case in North America, where conditions in the earliest nonnative settlements were not conducive to the establishment of printing presses and newspapers for some time. In rapid succession during the early 1600s, the English began a colony at Jamestown in the Chesapeake Bay (1607), the French built Quebec (1608), and the Dutch began exploring the region that became New York. Within another generation, the Plymouth Company (1620) and the Massachusetts Bay Company (1629) were also established. Building homes, establishing reliable sources of food and other basic necessities, and coping with harsh climates and disease were among the challenges faced by those who populated these settlements. Members of these communities also had to face problems that arose because they were encroaching on the homelands of native peoples who had lived there for millennia.

Primitive conditions and leadership problems caused the failure of the English settlement of Jamestown Colony. Established in 1607 by 105 men and boys, the site selected for the settlement was not a suitable one. Because it was located in a swamp, its soil was not fertile. Few of the colony's earliest inhabitants traveled to the New World to establish themselves in permanent homes, and they knew little about raising crops. Disease and malnutrition quickly took their toll. When supply ships arrived in January 1608, only 38 of the original group had escaped death. Despite such difficulties, however, roughly 500 new settlers arrived in the next several years. But disease, famine, and other hardships continued to plague the community, and by 1610, only about 60 of those who had settled there remained alive.

Writing later about Jamestown, John Smith reflected on the horrors endured by many of the community's inhabitants. He recalled, for example, how one man killed, salted, and ate his wife throughout one winter. Under Smith's leadership, the government declared martial law, executed whites who tried to escape to live with the Indians, and severely punished anyone who would not obey orders.[113]

It is easy to see that such living conditions rendered the establishment of printing offices, let alone the establishment of regularly published news, irrelevant. But even those who lived in America's cruelest frontier environments desired news of people and events outside their communities. As people crisscrossed the Appalachian Mountains to embark on new lives in the Kentucky country west of Virginia, they carried news-filled letters in both directions.[114] Handwritten newspapers were started in some communities before the arrival of printing presses.[115] And colonial Americans read and orally shared news they gleaned from papers imported from England and mainland Europe.

In addition to primitive living conditions, another factor in the slow growth of printed news in early America was the level of freedom authorities were willing to afford printers. For the most part, government leaders had little regard for printing presses. One of the Virginia Colony's royal governors, Sir William Berkeley, was responsible for the now-famous statement in his report to the Lords Commissioners of Foreign Plantations: "I thank God there are no free schools nor printing, and I hope we shall not have these hundred years; for learning has brought disobedience, and heresy and sects into the world, and printing has divulged them, . . . God keep us from both!"[116] When such an attitude at the top was coupled with the difficulties endured by Virginia's early settlers, it is not surprising that a printing press would not be installed in the territory until 1682.

Virginia's press was the second to be established in North America, the first having arrived at Cambridge, Massachusetts Bay Colony, in 1638. After Berkeley was replaced by a more lenient administrator, Lord Culpepper, the printer William Nuthead was invited to bring his press to the colony by John Buckner, a Gloucester County merchant and landowner. Official interference, however, led Nuthead to leave the colony rather quickly for Maryland, taking his press with him. After rumors of the existence of the press had reached the Virginia council, an investigation was launched, and Buckner and Nuthead were required to submit to questioning. At the end of the hearing, the council issued an order requiring Nuthead to pay a fine of one hundred pounds sterling and cease printing without preauthorization.[117]

Nuthead did not find the official climate for printing much improved in Maryland. Although the colony's leadership named him the public printer, the authorities still kept a close eye on what he issued from his press. In 1693, Nuthead was forced to defend himself against a charge that he had printed an illegal land warrant under the name of Lord Baltimore, who had recently lost title to such property. The council warned Nuthead that he should "print noethiing [sic] blank bills & Bonds, without leave from his Exncy or the further Order of this Board."

After Nuthead died in 1694, his wife, Dinah, took over the operation of the press after moving with the capital of colonial Maryland to Annapolis, thus becoming the first woman to operate a printing press in the colonies. Before setting to work, she was forced to petition the governor for a license and to pay a bond of one hundred pounds sterling to assure her good behavior in the operation of the press.

A society's literacy rate has been linked by some historians to to an increased likelihood of adopting print technologies and newspapers. This appears to be a reasonable conclusion, yet a closer look reveals a weaker association between the two developments than one might at first assume. Comparing literacy to the adoption of printing presses in different early American colonies offers a case in point. In one oft-cited study, Kenneth A. Lockridge compared the number of people who could sign their names on wills to those who signed their names with a mark. His findings indicated that 60 percent of New England white males leaving wills were literate in 1660. By 1710, the number had grown to 70 percent, and it rose to 85 percent by 1760. In contrast, literacy rates in seventeenth-century Virginia Colony were around 50 percent, rising to 66 percent in 1705 and 68 percent in 1762.[118]

Based on this comparison, is it safe to assume that New England's higher literacy rate led to an earlier establishment of printing presses and newspapers in that region? After all, Virginia lagged about fifty years behind New England in this respect. North America's first colonial printing press was started in Cambridge, Massachusetts, in 1638, and the country's first regularly published newspaper was begun in 1704 at Boston. In contrast, Virginia's first printing press did not arrive until 1682, and its first newspaper was not published until 1736. One might ask, therefore, if literacy was simply one indicator in a number of conditions that led to the establishment of North America's earliest printing press and newspaper in Massachusetts. Some would argue that Virginia's lack of public schools and the dispersed nature of its geographic settlement were also factors affecting people's attitudes about the adoption of printing presses and the establishment of local newspapers.

Those who settled Massachusetts Bay Colony were largely English Protestants whose concern for education coincided with their Puritan zeal for making sure everyone could read. Within a few years of founding the colony, officials enacted laws requiring schooling for all children. According to Harvey J. Graff, colonial New England's literacy rate rose from about one-half of all males in the middle of the seventeenth century to almost all men by the end of the eighteenth.[119]

In Virginia Colony, by contrast, schooling was not mandatory, and what schooling did exist was class-biased. This situation, when coupled with the low population density and the shorter life expectancy of southern settlers, meant there was less emphasis on literacy in Virginia than in New England.[120] Seventeenth-century Virginians could not expect to live to a ripe old age. At least 35,000 people migrated to the colony between 1607 and 1662, but the population in the latter year stood at only 25,600. By the middle of the century, the mortality rate had improved, but it still remained higher than that in New England. Many immigrants died within a year of arrival, victims of diseases to which they lacked immunity.[121]

In addition to society's overall living conditions and literacy rates, economic factors have affected the decisions printers and others interested in news dissemination have made about whether to adopt new technologies. Like all businesses, journalism is part of a broader economic system characterized by cycles beyond its control. During times of prosperity, news organizations' investments in new technologies have tended to increase, whereas economic panics and long-term depressions have undoubtedly had the reverse effect.

Since the turn of the nineteenth century, improvements in technologies had offered the publishers of newspapers opportunities to speed up their presses, produce better-looking publications, and cut their expenses for paper and ink. While newspapers in small towns and rural areas continued to operate their old presses, publishers in the population centers of New York and Philadelphia had more incentive to invest in new technologies.

Paper was always rare in early America. Indeed, until the first paper mill was built in Germantown, Pennsylvania, in 1690, it had to be imported. Paper was made from rags until well into the nineteenth century, and rags were always in short supply. More-over, papermaking was a laborious process, since every piece was made by hand. Eighteenth-century efforts to devise mechanized papermaking devices finally led to success, for in London in 1803, the Fourdrinier machine was built. First installed in London, the machine used a continuous roll of paper and was capable of de-livering sheets in specific sizes. Until the 1830s, only a few of these devices had been imported for use in the United States.

Prior to the early years of the nineteenth century, printer's ink had also been a constant problem for American newspaper pub-lishers. Most were forced to prepare their own ink, and quality varied greatly. In 1804, however, Jacob Johnson, of Philadelphia, set up an ink-supplying business that was large enough to provide inks on a commercial scale. In addition, improvements in ink making led to better results.

The most significant technological development during the early part of the nineteenth century was the improvement in the printing press. Up to that point, printers were still using the old screw presses that were based on Gutenberg's model. In 1813, however, George Clymer, another Philadelphian, perfected his Columbian press, which substituted a series of levers for the old single-screw device. But even though this machine was much easier and quicker to use, each printed piece was still created by hand. Friedrich Koenig's steam-powered printing press began to change that situation in 1810. While the type bed remained flat as in handpresses, the paper was pressed on the type by a cylinder. Then, in 1827, America's first steam-driven Koenig presses ar-rived. All publishers of the news undoubtedly admired these im-proved presses, yet only the owners of the wealthiest papers could afford to buy them. If money were no object, American journal-ists would likely have adopted steam-powered presses much more rapidly. But the financial realities early Americans publishers faced made that impossible. Although a few publishers became rich, most were unable to eke out more than a meager living from their newspapers.

In the eighteenth century, newspapers were but one of the various money-making activities printers engaged in. Newspapers alone would not sustain them, so they were also involved in such activities as job printing, the production and sale of legal and business forms, book printing and publishing, and the operation of bookstores. It was often difficult to get newspaper subscribers to pay their bills, and while advertising revenue helped a bit, some publishers were always on the edge of bankruptcy. As one editor from Trenton, New Jersey, put it in his newspaper, the *True American:* "We do not believe there is any trade or calling in the Union that involves those who pursue it in equal trouble and expense with that of News-paper printing, & at the same time gives them such small profits and poor pay."[122]

Financial cycles of boom and bust added to the economic woes of America's early newspaper publishers. In 1819, the country's first major economic panic hit with a vengeance that spared neither rich nor poor. Although the economy had long suffered from periodic financial instabilities, this situation was unprecedented. It seemed to have come from nowhere, as no particular event, leader, or act of government could be pinned with the blame. Mathew Carey estimated that three million people, one-third of the country's population, were directly affected by the panic. The number of bankruptcies climbed, prices dropped, unemployment increased, foreclosures multiplied, and investments and property values plunged. Mounting numbers of people were sent to debtors' prisons, and urban poverty became so severe that it was impossible for city authorities to ignore it.

Whether publishers of newspapers were severely hit by the dire economic problems of that period is unclear, although it is probable that anyone who had considered purchasing faster presses before the panic would have been forced to abandon such plans. Faster presses were available by 1819, but most of America's newspapers were still produced on the same old machines that had been used for generations. Circulation of some the newspapers in the nation's urban centers had been slowly growing, along with the overall numbers of papers published. But the old presses could keep up with the demands of the day, meaning there was little pressure to invest in the faster printers that were available.

One discernible effect of the panic was that it put pressure on newspaper editors to improve their papers' coverage of economic news. Up to that point, America's newspapers did not yet have a clearly defined role as purveyors of news on financial matters, and most journalists had little experience reporting on economic panic. But editors responded admirably by publishing large numbers of reports and essays on the conditions experienced by Americans during the crisis. Newspaper columnists also sought answers to questions about the origins of the panic, and they searched for remedies for the extreme hardships experienced by so many people. The author of a series of columns published in 1818 and 1819 in the *National Advocate,* for example, blamed three things for the hard times: unwise speculations, overspending, and the extravagance of society's women.[123]

Another major panic hit in 1837, with even worse effects than the 1819 event. Economic historians regard this second panic as one of America's worst economic depressions, rivaled only by the twentieth century's Great Depression. The panic was born of years of inflationary overspeculation, and when the bubble burst in New York City, every bank immediately stopped payment in specie (gold and silver coinage). The panic was followed by a five-year depression that brought with it the failure of many banks and record unemployment levels.

The economic panic of 1837 hit just after a small group of New York City newspaper entrepreneurs had started to invest in faster printing presses to help boost the circulations of their penny papers. Until the 1830s, hand-operated presses functioned at a top rate of three hundred impressions an hour. But based on the model of a popular London newspaper that catered to working-class readers and cost only a penny, printer Benjamin H. Day started the *New York Sun* in 1833. To succeed, Day had to sell a lot of newspapers, and from the start, it was evident that he would have no trouble in doing so. Within four months, the *Sun*'s circulation was 4,000. By late 1834, Day had invested in a new press capable of 1,000 impressions per hour, and this boosted the paper's circulation to more than 10,000. Another new press in 1835 increased the *Sun*'s capacity to 22,000, and the paper was enlarged to a fourteen-by-twenty-inch size in 1836.

Day's newspaper was especially vulnerable to the panic's effects because so many of its readers were from low-income groups. A period of declining sales and advertising revenues just after the panic forced Day to sell his property to his brother-in-law, the paper manufacturer Moses Y. Beach, for $40,000. Beach had more capital to invest in the *Sun,* and he immediately purchased the most advanced printing technology of the day, a steam-driven Hoe cylinder press capable of producing 4,000 papers an hour.[124]

It took five years for the United States to fully recover from the effects of the panic of 1837, and while the country's economy went through periodic growth and contraction cycles thereafter, it was not until the 1930s that newspapers would once again experience a severe decline in circulation. The Great Depression and the growing popularity of radio led to these problems, and in the 1950s, television made things worse. During the 1960s and 1970s, changing demographics caused even more problems for newspapers. As people moved to the suburbs, city papers lost readers, and the population as a whole increased its consumption of radio and television news. The afternoon newspaper disappeared from most markets, and adverse inheritance tax policies made it difficult for family-owned newspaper businesses to be passed on without going public.

All these changes paved the way for outside investors to buy more and more papers, and in hopes of winning back readers, they invested, among other things, in innovative technologies that could deliver more vibrant, exciting news products. The purchase of color presses was one strategy increasingly employed by newspapers after 1982, when *USA Today* introduced color into America's major markets. The costs involved in installing color presses were exorbitant, so those publishers who did so wanted to make an impression. In a 1984 *Newsweek* article, critic Jerry Adler wrote that the Los Angeles Olympics in that year was offering the *Los Angeles Times* an opportunity to impress not only local people but also those who traveled from across the globe to attend the games. As he put it: "For the *Times* the Olympics were an irresistible opportunity to show off its star writers, its new color and its enormous depth. . . . It was, over all, a bravura demonstration of what a newspaper can accomplish."[125]

Some papers returned to prosperity, at least for a while. But as more papers invested in color, competition once again led to declines in profit. In the 1990s, the *Hackensack Record,* one of New Jersey's leading midsize papers and one of the prior decade's early adopters of color presses and other expansion programs, once again fell on hard times. *Washington Post* columnist Howard Kurtz

wrote: "The forces that have buffeted the paper are all too familiar. . . . In the face of the industry's declining readership rates, vir-
tually all newspapers are trying to reinvent themselves, and many
see their salvation in low-cal journalism topped with color pictures
and fancy graphics."[126]

In addition to society's living conditions, support or lack of support for press freedom, literacy rates, and cycles of economic boom
and bust, the operators of America's news organizations have also
contended with the unexpected effects of wars. During periods of
conflict, American newspeople have stopped conducting business
as usual and done whatever they could to bring their readers news
of the battles and other military matters. Such demands have made
wars particularly fertile periods for the adoption or increased of use
of technologies that could help journalists better serve the needs of
the public.

The first major war that involved the American colonies was
the 1754–1763 French and Indian War. Benjamin Franklin has
been credited with publishing America's first newspaper political
cartoon during this period. The cartoon appeared in his paper, the
Pennsylvania Gazette, in 1754, under the caption "Join or Die."
Franklin's cartoon was used by other newspaper printers and was
brought to life again during the 1765 Stamp Act crisis and the
Revolutionary War.

After the Revolution, the next major conflict the United
States became involved in was the 1801–1805 Tripolitan War.
The war front was the coast of Africa in the Mediterranean, and
the enemies were the Barbary States of Morocco, Algiers, Tripoli,
and Tunisia. The dispute is often overlooked in histories of
America, even though it marked the first time the country's
troops fought on foreign soil. It started when U.S. officials refused
to meet the demands of Barbary pirates who regularly stopped

ships and demanded tribute for the right to sail in territory they sought to control. In the process, the pirates captured sailors and put them into slavery, thereby putting more pressure on officials to meet their demands.

Up to that point, many countries, including the United States, had paid off the pirates. Indeed, by 1801, American officials had given them nearly $2 million in tribute. When Thomas Jefferson was sworn in as America's new president in March 1801, he was immediately forced to decide whether the nation should continue to pay the pirates. Even though he was averse to doing so, he ultimately chose to send naval captain William Bainbridge to the Mediterranean with money to pay off the dey of Algiers. After an unexpected turn of events, Tripoli declared war on the United States on June 10, 1801.

Because newspapers did not yet have a tradition of sending correspondents to cover wartime events and because the telegraph was not yet invented, Tripolitan War–era editors depended on letters sent home by naval leaders and sailors for news of the conflict. The letters and dispatches that contained information on the war often took weeks and at times months to be delivered. Out of these reports came thrilling stories about the exploits of some of the nation's earliest heroes.

Since technologies that would have enabled journalists to print photographs or broadcast live images would not be available for generations, Americans tended to romanticize the war's events and heroes. Always looking for ways to make money, printers responded by publishing pamphlets, books, and even musical scores that glamorized the war's most famous battles and protagonists. The story of the U.S. Marines' assault on Tripoli, for example, was printed after being set to music by composer Benjamin Carr in *The Siege of Tripoli: An Historical Naval Sonata for the Piano Forte.*

On June 18, 1812, the United States declared war on Great Britain. For two years, the countries were locked in a series of battles that led to few gains on either side. The War of 1812 was one of the most unpopular conflicts in American history. When a treaty was signed on December 24, 1814, diplomats agreed that the countries should return to the situations they were in before hostilities erupted. Throughout the war, American news publishers were constantly reminded of the slowness of the day's major communication vehicles—the mails and shipping. And never was this situation more frustrating than during the days before, during, and after the burning of Washington, D.C., by British troops on August 24, 1814.

As the enemy advanced on Washington, rumors that its troops were heading in the direction of the capital led to panic. The editors of the *National Intelligencer* attempted to placate their readers with promises that they would provide the most up-to-date and dependable information available. In an August 20 column titled "The Enemy," they vowed to sort fact from fiction. They wrote: "We shall lose no time in publishing such intelligence of the enemy's movements as they may safely be relied on. In the present state of things, however, the various rumors that will be daily circulated should be received with caution."

Despite growing evidence that Washington was on the verge of being attacked, American military leaders failed to prepare for the assault, and when British troops arrived at the city, there were only a few local militia there to defend it. As the city burned, British troops dined at the president's table and selected souvenirs from his home's furnishings. After twenty-six hours at the capital, the British headed for Baltimore, where their attacks two weeks later inspired Francis Scott Key to write "The Star Spangled Banner." Accounts of the sacking of the nation's capital traveled slowly in the days and weeks that followed. Residents of Philadelphia, which was 126 miles from Washington, would not receive news of the event until twenty-four hours later. New York City residents would not get the news for another day, and it took a week for the story of the capital's devastation to reach Raleigh, North Carolina.

Complicating the spread of news during this period was the destruction of the offices of the *National Intelligencer*. The editors, who promised to remain in the capital as long as it was safe to do so, had only just escaped when British rear admiral George Cockburn arrived at their office. Cockburn intended to burn the *Intelligencer*'s building. He was aware of the paper's critical stance on the British and was especially infuriated by the fact that one of its editors, Joseph Gales Jr., was a native of England. After being talked out of burning the building by its adjoining occupants, Cockburn ordered his troops to destroy the paper's equipment, materials, and library.

The War of 1812 reinforced people's awareness that news delivery was often so slow that it led to problems. But the situation during the Civil War marked the strides made in communication technologies in the intervening years. The harnessing of the telegraph by an enterprising group of newspaper publishers in 1846 meant that journalistic coverage of the Civil War was much faster and more complete than was possible during the War of 1812. The Civil War was also critical in the history of the technologies of journalism because of the increasing use newspaper publishers were making of recent advances in printing and visual technologies.

During the war, the daily Northern press supplied its readers with an unprecedented number of maps portraying the conflict's battles, campaigns, and scenes of operations. The more than two thousand maps published in Northern papers from 1861 to 1865 gave the public never-before-experienced access to military intelligence. In fact, maps based on military secrets sometimes appeared in the papers even before they arrived in Washington. Some were based on eyewitness sketches delivered by correspondents attached to battlefield armies.[127]

The already popular illustrated newspaper flourished during the Civil War, and newspapers not previously notable for copious visual news treatments used such technologies more and more. In addition, the increasing numbers of newspaper illustrations seen during the war were used to convey more than battlefield and military news. In New York City, the public desire for diversion was extreme, and the city's newspaper editors used the day's popular visual technologies to meet this need. On February 10, 1863, in the midst of the Civil War, a happening of great interest took place in New York City. As one *New York Observer* writer commented: "It is the event of the century, if not unparalleled in history." And a *New York Times* columnist wrote it was "an event unprecedented, and as pregnant with study for the scientific, as with wonder for the million."[128] What the scribblers were writing about was the marriage of the wildly popular midget and longtime P. T. Barnum protégé General Tom Thumb to Lavinia Warren, another little person recently employed by the showman.

The press covered every imaginable detail of the couple's elaborate wedding, reception, and honeymoon tour, and the public's favorable reaction suggests the story helped dispel some of the gloom of the dreadful winter of 1863. Part of what the public enjoyed was the press's use of illustrations. Barnum employed Mathew Brady as the couple's wedding photographer, and after the event, he sold thousands of *cartes de visites* as souvenirs. All this helped precipitate a shift in the budding field of photography and in the news media more generally. Brady had made it his mission to, in his own words, "preserve the faces of its historic men and mothers."[129] Increasingly during the Civil War, he and his cadre of photographers captured event-centered scenes, and the Thumb-Warren wedding was part of this development.

With the advent of a halftone screening process, which was patented in 1881, newspapers were given a valuable tool with which to report the Spanish-American War of 1898. The process made it possible to publish photographic images, rather than renderings of such images, in newspapers and magazines. By the late 1880s, *Frank Leslie's Illustrated Newspaper* and *Harper's Weekly* included halftones. By the time the war began, American newspapers and magazines were liberally reproducing them along with the engraved images they still published. As one scholar stated: "The invention of the halftone ushered in the first 'living-room war.'"[130] Most of the halftones that accompanied the war's combat stories appeared singly rather than in groups. *Collier's,* however, eventually began to arrange images in groups with brief captions.

Wars are not the only crises that have affected how technologies have been used for news dissemination. Disasters have likewise captured the attention of the public, and journalists have responded by using the most effective technologies available to provide the fastest and most complete news coverage possible. The unpredictability of nature has always exposed humans to the dangers of storms, earthquakes, volcanoes, landslides, tsunamis, floods, droughts, epidemics, and sudden infestations of deadly insects or animals. Other disasters, such as the 1912 sinking of the *Titanic* and nuclear accidents at Three Mile Island in 1984 and Chernobyl in 1986, are attributable to human error and/or technical malfunctions. That disasters, even today, can so quickly transform stable communities into uninhabitable or unsafe wastelands puts them high on the list of public concerns.

People began communicating news of disasters in oral tales and ballads about fierce storms, epidemics, and earthquakes. After the advent of printing, some of these accounts were reproduced in pamphlets, newspapers, and books. In 1692, an anonymous London printer published a news sheet titled *A True and Impartial Account, of the Strange and Wonderful Earthquake, Which Happened in Most Parts of the City . . . the Eighth of September, 1692*. Twelve years later, Daniel Defoe published his first book, *The Storm*, a journalistic account of the "remarkable casualties and disasters" that hit Great Britain when a hurricane made it across the Atlantic to the British Isles.[131] A decade later, his famous *Journal of the Plague Year* was published. Even though it was not revealed in his account of the epidemic that he himself did not live through it, the book is still considered a major work in the early history of the field of literary journalism.

Early American journalists also published pamphlets and newspaper reports about disasters they learned of through eyewitness or secondhand accounts. When the first steamboat to travel down the Ohio and Mississippi rivers left Pittsburgh on October 20, 1811, no one imagined the voyage would become famous for reasons beyond the history of transportation. A number of unusual things happened as the boat made its way to New Orleans, including the Great Madrid Earthquake. Printed accounts of the boat's journey and the quake were published after the boat arrived at New Orleans.

Deadly storms also captured the imaginations of Americans. The day after a tremendous storm hit Providence, Rhode Island, Thomas Bennet Smith authored a newspaper story that not only gave an account of the damage caused by the storm that had just happened but also reminisced about a big storm that hit the city in 1815.[132]

In the twentieth century, the role of disasters in the process whereby technologies became intertwined with news production continued. On April 14, 1912, the world's largest passenger liner, the *Titanic,* sank after hitting an iceberg in the North Atlantic. Of the ship's 2,227 passengers, only 705 survived. The disaster been described as one of the century's most important news stories, and it has also been linked to the history of radio broadcasting.[133] Immediately after the *Titanic* hit the iceberg, a Morse light was used to signal for help, and one of the ship's wireless operators started sending out SOS messages. Although it is not clear that the ship's signal was heard in New York City, a young Marconi Wireless Telegraph Company employee, David Sarnoff, became involved in the unfolding drama as word of it spread. For three days and nights, he sat at his post as a wireless telegraph operator, and in return for his service, he was named chief inspector for Marconi's nationwide facilities.

There is a connection between the *Titanic,* Sarnoff, and the growth of the idea that radio ought to be used for broadcasting. Although Reginald A. Fessenden and others had been experimenting with radio broadcasting since at least 1906, Sarnoff's ability to get people excited about radio broadcasting was unmatched. In November 1916, he wrote what is now a famous memo, proposing that radio should be used primarily for broadcasting rather than point-to-point communication. The wireless, he suggested, could be used to send signals that could be received by a "Radio Music Box." People could buy this device for use in their kitchens and living rooms. Headphones would not be necessary, since radio boxes would have loudspeakers that would pipe music and other audio programming into the room. Although the government put a hold on the broadcasting of messages during World War I,

Sarnoff's idea began to take off as soon as the treaty ending the war was signed.

Much more recently, two natural disasters have led to an increased use of the Weblog, or blog as it is generally called, for news dissemination. Blogs are journals that are frequently updated and are intended for public consumption. They generally represent the personality of the author or the Web site and, while there have always been bloggers with an interest in publishing the news, blogs are primarily used to communicate opinions. Since it became possible for nonexperts to create blogs free of charge in 1999, the practice has grown so quickly that blogging is generally referred to as a revolution. A number of the blogosphere's most notable contributors emigrated from the world of mainstream journalism, and the unorthodox news-writing practices of some have led to a great deal of criticism.

News events that have become milestones in the young history of blogging have often related to politics. But since late 2004, two disasters with cataclysmic effects have put the role of the blogosphere as an important disseminator of news and information in the limelight. The first took place on December 24, 2004, when a tsunami that devastated coastal areas in Indonesia, Malaysia, Thailand, Myanmar, India, the Maldives, Sri Lanka, and Somalia was produced by a magnitude 9.0 earthquake 155 kilometers southwest of northern Sumatra. The tsunami inundated those coastal areas with waves more than thirty feet high every thirty to forty minutes for several hours. The disaster resulted in the deaths of more than one hundred and fifty thousand people and injured millions.

Since there was no warning before the waves hit, the world's news community was forced to scramble to cover the disaster. And in addition to those outside the devastation who wanted to hear about what had happened, people in the vicinity of the affected areas were in desperate need of information. Bloggers stepped in to help fill the news and information gap. In May 2005, Miguel Ramos and Paul S. Piper wrote: "The tsunami of Dec. 26, 2004, has become another defining moment in the evolution and use of blogs. These distributed, interactive resources rallied around the disaster in ways that allowed readers to learn of the disaster, find ways to help through direct donations or volunteer opportunities, and cope with the grief that such an event inevitably brings."[134]

Less than a year later, Hurricane Katrina also became a factor in the developing role of Weblogs as communicators of news. After forming over the Bahamas on August 23, 2005, the storm crossed southern Florida before moving into the Gulf of Mexico. Gathering strength, it eventually moved ashore along the Gulf Coast on August 29. The hurricane was so massive that it caused extensive damages many miles from its center. The storm surge caused from major to catastrophic destruction along the coastlines of Louisiana, Mississippi, and Alabama, including the cities of Mobile in Alabama, Gulfport and Biloxi in Mississippi, and Slidell in Louisiana. The surge also caused the failure of the levees that were intended to keep the waters of Lake Pontchartrain from flooding New Orleans. Roughly 80 percent of the city was flooded, along with extensive areas within neighboring parishes. More than seventeen hundred deaths resulted from the storm and its aftermath, although the exact toll is unknown because some bodies were never found.

With several days of advance warning about an event that took place right at home, mainstream journalists were in a much better position to cover Katrina than they were the tsunamis. But within days of the event, commentary cropped up about the pivotal role bloggers were taking in the dissemination of Katrina-related news and information. On September 1, an *Information Week* article stated: "Bloggers and other citizen journalists have once again proven the growing importance of the Internet in covering the biggest news events, contributing heart-wrenching, personal accounts in living the tragedy from Hurricane Katrina." In the same article, CNN.com's executive vice president, Mitch Gelman, was quoted as stating: "Traditional journalism is the outside looking in. Citizen journalism is the inside looking out. In order to get the complete story, it helps to have both points of view."[135]

Such perspectives are indicative of the impact blogging technology is having on the practice of gathering and distributing news. Although the history of blogging has only just begun, the phenomenon of the news blogger represents a return to the old idea of the citizen journalist. The editors of America's earliest newspapers depended heavily on letters and essays sent by members of the public who were in a position to observe and write about events that took place outside their immediate communities. Despite the fact that many of today's mainstream news editors have little respect for the work of bloggers, it is likely that this new technology will continue to have an impact into the future.

The history of journalism is littered with the relics of news forms and delivery systems that failed because they did not become popular or, after a period of popularity, were supplanted by others that outshone them. In addition, people involved in the development of emerging news technologies have sometimes tried to bring them to a public that was not ready to accept them for one reason or another. A focus on the stories of several of these journalistic dinosaurs and "inventions before their times" reveals the complexity of the dynamics of change. In certain cases, technologies alone seem to be the primary driving force behind the abandonment of particular news vehicles. But in other instances, social, cultural, economic, geographic, or political factors offer a better vantage point from which to view the dynamics of change within journalism.

At certain times, the appearance of a new technology has meant the quick demise of an older one. An excellent example is journalists' abrupt abandonment of an earlier news delivery system— that which depended on the horse for transportation. Horses have been involved in the delivery of news since their domestication, but in 1860, a trio of freight and storage operators concocted a plan to harness their potential in a more systematic way. That April, William H. Russell, William B. Waddell, and Alexander Majors started the pony express, a news delivery system that, for a short time, solved a communication problem no technology of the day could handle. The three businessmen appreciated the fact that the impending Civil War had spurred the need for faster news delivery across the great expanses of the western territory. Since neither the railroad nor the telegraph yet spanned the country, the transmission of news across the Great Plains and mountains of the West took months.

The teams of pony riders hired by the new company's directors cut the time needed to get news across the country considerably. On April 3, 1860, the first teams of pony express riders were sent out simultaneously from St. Joseph, Missouri, and Sacramento, California. The first westbound trip of the service was made in nine days and twenty-three hours, while those traveling eastbound rode for a total of eleven days and twelve hours. The express's speediest run, which involved the delivery of President Abraham Lincoln's inaugural address, was seven days and seventeen hours. Another piece of important news that reached California via the pony express was the outbreak of the Civil War;

some have credited the express with helping to keep California in the Union. For eighteen months, the approximately eighty to one hundred riders hired by the company logged six hundred and fifty thousand miles in their runs across the country. Though their trips were sometimes hazardous, historians claim only one delivery was lost.

The pony express disappeared in the blink of an eye in October 1861. The demise of the company had nothing to do with a decreased need for news from the East, however; if anything, in the midst of the Civil War, people's need for news was more intense than ever before. The express was no longer needed because a more efficient news delivery system replaced it when the Pacific Telegraph Company completed its line to San Francisco. A *California Pacific* writer acknowledged the service's obsolescence: "A fast and faithful friend has the pony been to our far off state. Summer and winter, storm and shine, day and night, he has traveled like a weaver's shuttle back and forth 'till now his work is done. Goodbye, Pony. . . . You have served us well."[136]

An example of a technology-based news form that did not immediately thrive because of contextual factors that temporarily dampened the public's response to it was the battlefield image. Americans were hungry for the wildly popular *cartes de visites* and stereo cards of the day, but battlefield images taken by Alexander Gardner and put on display in Mathew Brady's New York Gallery in 1862 "literally stunned the American people" because of their realistic portrayal of the horrible costs of war.[137]

Titled "The Dead of Antietam," the exhibit received a great deal of attention. Brady offered these images for sale at his gallery and reproduced them as wood engravings in *Harper's Weekly.* Brady also reproduced the Antietam photographs as stereo cards, a type of photograph that would remain popular for decades. He and the other photographers of the day had better luck selling photographic portraits of well-known people such as Abraham Lincoln, Ulysses S. Grant, and Tom Thumb and his bride, Lavinia. Among the most sought-after photographs during the Civil War were the daguerreotypes and *cartes de visites* that were sold at prices almost anyone could afford. During the war, people enjoyed purchasing and assembling them into albums to be shared with family and friends.

The public was not ready for Brady's expansive vision of the potential of photography. Clearly, he saw that the images he captured through his lens had the power to change history. A supporter of the Republican Party, Brady created thirty-five portraits of Abraham Lincoln during the 1860 presidential election. After his victory, Lincoln told his friends: "Brady and the Cooper Union speech made me President."[138]

Brady's Civil War photographs were starkly different from the ones he and his assistants took in his studios. After the war broke out, his business quickly became intertwined with the conflict. Many Union soldiers and officers wanted to be photographed in uniform before they left home, and in July 1861, Brady and Alfred Waud, a *Harper's Weekly* artist, traveled to the front line and witnessed Bull Run, the first major battle of the war and a disaster for the Union. Brady came close to being captured by the enemy.

On his return, Brady devoted himself to creating a photographic record of the war. He financed an expedition involving more than twenty photographers and assistants who traveled across the country taking pictures at the war's camps and battlegrounds. Over the course of the project, Brady spent $100,000 to obtain about ten thousand prints. Unable to acquire a government subsidy to help recoup the large sum of money he had invested in the enterprise, he opened his Antitetam exhibition. Some of the pictures taken at the bloody battle portrayed scenes with corpses and other graphic material.

Considering that the public was desperate for news of the war and that it had generally responded quite favorably to his other work, Brady must have been flummoxed by its reaction to his new exhibit. Most of those who viewed his pictures were witnessing the carnage of the war for the first time in their lives, and their reactions were somber and anything but congratulatory in the recognition that Brady had broken new ground. A *New York Times* reporter wrote:

> The dead of the battle-field come up to us very rarely, even in dreams. We see the list in the morning paper at breakfast, but dismiss its recollection with the coffee. There is a confused mass of names, but they are all strangers; we forget the horrible significance that dwells amid the jumble of type. . . . We recognize the battle-field as a reality, but it stands as a remote one. It is like a funeral next door. It attracts your attention, but it does not enlist your sympathy. But it is very different when the hearse stops at your front door and the corpse is carried over your own threshold. . . . Mr. Brady has done something to bring to us the terrible reality and earnestness of the War. If he has not brought bodies and laid them in our door-yards and along [our] streets, he has done something very like it.

The relative lack of interest in Brady's Civil War images may have stemmed, in part, from the fact that few could attend his gallery shows or could afford the limited-edition books of photos he was selling. If Brady's efforts to gain appreciation for some of history's earliest photojournalistic images had been more successful, it is possible that the history of visual news would have advanced more quickly. But mitigating against the development of popular appreciation for images that brought the news of the day to life were the era's social and cultural values. Brady's role as one of photojournalism's earliest innovators is largely recognized today. But not until the Spanish-American War and the Progressive Era would the field of photojournalistic news advance more quickly.

Although we've only recently entered the computer age, history has already been witness to a number of its failed news experiments. One of them was the videotex, a system that uses telephone lines to send pages of text in computer form to be displayed on individuals' televisions. The first attempt to establish a videotex system was made in the United Kingdom in the late 1960s. Following this, journalists quickly saw the potential videotex held for the dissemination of news, and in 1970, the BBC started researching how it could employ the technology to send closed-captioning information. Two years later, the BBC decided not to limit videotex to closed captioning, and in 1972, it launched the first public manifestation of the project under the name Ceefax. Investors in videotex realized that they might be able to exploit a market hungry for information and data services related to banking, travel, and traffic conditions. In addition, research indicated people would be interested in receiving traditional newspaper content over videotex.

Meanwhile, in the United Kingdom, Japan, Europe, Canada, and the United States, a variety of entrepreneurs were following these developments with interest. On August 16, 1978, an article in the *Citizen,* a newspaper in Ottawa, Canada, predicted that by the early 1980s, the public would receive electronic mail delivery, news coverage, and myriad "entertaining pastimes" over videotex. Its author wrote: "Hundreds of mailmen, paperboys, and information service people will be put out of work by the [videotex] service. But a viable industry, employing about 32,000 people, is expected to evolve with the network."

One of the earliest companies in America to invest in videotex's potential was Radio Shack, which attempted to sell its brand of terminals to consumers across the country. Although sales were low, several U.S.-based media firms, including Knight-Ridder, the *Los Angeles Times,* and Field Enterprises in Chicago, started their own videotex projects in the early 1980s. By the middle of the decade, however, all of these efforts had ended in failure, the primary problems being that the systems were expensive and their performance was slow and cumbersome. Adding to these problems was the fact that, unlike the situation in the United Kingdom, where videotex signals were free, American customers were forced to pay hundreds of dollars for the installation of videotex equipment, along with high monthly service fees for receiving videotex signals.

The inability of videotex's investors to interest the public in the technology as a news form demonstrates that the novelty attached to a particular innovation is sometimes not enough to assure its success. Along with Mathew Brady's failure to interest the public in his Antietam photographs, this example serves to remind us that those who promote the use of technologies ahead of their time will rarely gain widespread acceptance. Clearly, proponents of emerging technologies for journalistic purposes must compete against already successful ones, and beyond that, they must also confront social realities and cultural values.

FOUR

MORE AND MORE NEWS

A great admirer of newspapers, Mark Twain once commented: "The old saw says, 'Let a sleeping dog lie.' Right! Still, when there is much at stake it is better to get a newspaper to do it."[139] Twain's sentiments aptly captured the spirit of the nineteenth century, a period historians often refer to as the golden age of American newspapers. Until the emergence of radio in the 1920s, the printing press and its newspapers reigned supreme in the practice of journalism. Papers were society's major source of nonoral news, and they also grew in number, size, circulation, categories, and geographic range. Manufacturers of printing presses invested their time and money in projects to improve their machines: the telegraph led to faster and wider availability of news, and the halftone led the way to the flowering of the field of photojournalism. But improvements in technology alone do not explain these changes. Americans' intense interest in politics and the cultural concerns for expansionism, evangelicalism, and reform all played pivotal roles in the growth of the newspaper in the nineteenth century.

One way to gauge a burgeoning news culture is by the number of newspapers and other forms of news in existence. America's census of newspapers did not increase greatly from 1704 to the American Revolution. Of the thirty-five published at the start of the war, only twenty survived at its conclusion. Yet even though they were few in number, small, and often crudely produced, both Tory and patriot papers were crucial providers of information and moral support, and some of those that survived the war had grown in circulation.

A publisher of a newspaper that did grow was Isaiah Thomas, one of America's most famous patriot printers. Thomas established the *Massachusetts Spy* in Boston in 1770. After suffering through four years of serious threats from the colonial government, including being burned in effigy, Thomas gave his paper a new masthead representing a dragon and snake about to engage in conflict. The illustration was modeled after the woodcut cartoon Benjamin Franklin published in 1754 under the caption "Join or Die." After being forced to close the *Spy* in 1775, Thomas secretly transported his printing press fifty miles west to Worcester and reopened it under the title the *Massachusetts Spy or Oracle of American Liberty.*

Americans' experiences with newspapers such as Thomas's *Massachusetts Spy* fostered a greater appreciation for them than had existed before the Revolution. From the conclusion of the war to 1800, their numbers increased from twenty to about two hundred. Following the turn of the century, multiple factors contributed to an even more dramatic growth of the newspaper industry. By 1900, their numbers total more than eleven thousand. America's earliest newspapers were started in coastal towns such as Boston; Providence, Rhode Island; Portsmouth, New Hampshire; New York City; Annapolis and Baltimore, Maryland; Portland, Maine; Wilmington, North Carolina; and Charleston, South Carolina. Philadelphia and Hartford, Connecticut, also became important centers for newspaper publishing in the colonial era. After the Revolution, printers took their presses over the Appalachian Mountains into the Northwest Territory, down to Florida, and across the South. Everywhere they went, they established newspapers.

One center of noticeable growth in the newspaper business at the turn of the nineteenth century was Washington, D.C., which had replaced Philadelphia as the nation's permanent capital in 1801. Seven newspapers were started in Georgetown and Washington, on the Potomac, in 1800. In 1791, former president George Washington had selected a site for the capital near the village of Georgetown, which had been laid out and incorporated in 1789. In 1794, construction of the nation's new capitol building began, but the place remained relatively quiet until government officials started arriving in the summer of 1800 for the first session of Congress, scheduled to begin that fall. Americans were curious about the new capital, and the newspapers kept them informed. Descriptions of the nascent federal city, along with commentary on its living conditions, were common additions to papers throughout the country.

As the country's population centers expanded after the Revolution, so did the number of newspapers. Printers had only attempted to establish a total of eight newspapers in the fledgling town of New York from 1704 to 1765, but by 1850, the city had become the newspaper capital of the world. The number of copies of papers published in New York each day at midcentury demonstrated the high regard New Yorkers had for them. While London, the world's other great newspaper city, surpassed New York in the number of papers published in 1850—144 compared to 106—the total number of copies circulated each day in New York City was far higher. In 1850, New Yorkers purchased about 153,000 papers each day, whereas Londoners purchased about 63,000. In 1898, Joseph Pulitzer's *World* alone had a daily circulation of 1.3 million.[140]

The country's newspapers not only increased in number over the decades of the nineteenth century but also grew in size. The first colonial papers were printed on small single sheets. Later in the century and through the Revolutionary War era, they were enlarged and often consisted of four pages of three-column type. By 1800, many were printed on even larger sheets, and five columns were common. During the 1830s and 1840s, especially in the nation's booming urban centers, newspaper publishers started another enlargement trend, marked by bigger pages accommodating six columns of type. During the post–Civil War era, the dimensions of many newspapers became even larger, with the number of columns growing in some cases up to eight and even ten.

Although the term *manifest destiny* was not coined until 1845, Americans had long before displayed a healthy urge to move into the nation's southern and western frontiers. The flatbed press, which had not changed much since Gutenberg's time, was easy to load on wagons or boats for the long trips across mountains and plains. The first newspaper started west of the Appalachian Mountains was John Scull's venture of 1786, the *Pittsburgh Gazette.* A year later, John Bradford set up shop in Lexington, Kentucky, and established that territory's first newspaper, the *Lexington Gazette.* The first newspaper to be published in the Northwest Territory, the *Centinel,* was started in 1793. By 1800, the twenty-one papers published beyond the Appalachian Mountains were indicators of a new and soon-to-be-thriving frontier press. The first newspaper published west of the Mississippi was started in St. Louis in 1808, when the city's population was less than five hundred.

Although the papers in the West's fledgling communities were often crudely printed, Americans considered them to be essential signifiers of progress. Everyone who could wield a pen was urged to contribute material for the papers, and government officials at

times wrote for them as well. Lively exchanges on issues of importance to the community were printed in the papers. Politics was a
favorite topic, but so were pieces on the expanding fields of transportation, farming, and mechanics. By midcentury, the western
newspaper symbolized the country's twin spirits of expansionism
and entrepreneurialism.

A desire for economic growth among the Americans who
moved to the western and southern frontiers led them to use the
newspapers in an effort to attract additional settlers to their towns.
In his study of the growth of Chicago, environmental historian
William Cronon noted that boosters believed "climate, soils, veg-
etation, transportation routes, and other features of the landscape
all pointed toward key locations that nature had designated for
urban greatness."[141]

To help their nascent communities achieve the "urban greatness" the citizens hoped for, newspapers kept their readers informed about the progress they were making. In 1858, a pair of
immigrant brothers, Alexander and William Kinkaid, sought to
build a town in the wilds of Minnesota. After arriving in Douglas
County, in the state's north-central lake region, they built a log
cabin. Next, they secured the services of a government surveyor,
who helped them survey and plat a town site. After naming their
new town Alexandria, they built a log hotel, established a post office, and opened a road to the north. To attract settlers, the
Kinkaid brothers sent word back to the newspapers in St. Paul,
and by 1860, Douglas County had 196 inhabitants. A paper
named the *Alexandria Post* was established in 1868, and its editors,
W. Benedict and William E. Hicks, periodically inserted reports
in its pages on how the town was progressing. On January 7,
1876, a front-page *Post* article, under the headline THE GROWTH
OF ALEXANDRIA, reviewed the town's expansion over the

previous year and discussed the editors' hopes for progress in the year to come.

Before moving to Alexandria, Hicks had served as the *New-York Evening Post*'s financial editor. He moved to Minnesota because he believed its clean and invigorating air would help him overcome tuberculosis. Hicks may have heard about Minnesota's "enervating prairies" in one of James M. Goodhue's newspaper columns, which were sent to the East from time to time. Goodhue was the publisher of one of Minnesota's first newspapers, the *Minnesota Pioneer*. In an early issue of his paper, he printed a long piece on the virtues of St. Anthony, the village that would later become Minneapolis. Part of the piece touched on the territory's climate: "What is fertility, what is wealth, without vigorous health and activity of body and of mind? These are considerations that will weigh more in future with the immigrants, than they hitherto have: a clear, bracing air, an invigorating winter to give elasticity to the system—and water as pure and soft as the dews of heaven, gushing from hill and valley."[142] The newspapers that contained these articles were sent eastward, and when they were out of print, Goodhue republished them to meet the demand.

Goodhue's statements about Minnesota's climate were meant to convince those heading west that the territory's environment was not as harsh as they thought. Editors of various Great Plains newspapers sought to dispel the common notion that the country west of the Mississippi was largely a dry and inhospitable desert. In 1892, when land in west-central Oklahoma was opened for settlement, the town of Arapaho was founded. A few days later, Frank Fillmore and William Seaman started a newspaper for the express purpose of "booming" the region. In the first issue of their paper, the *Arrow*, the editors wrote: "If you want to settle in one of the most prosperous counties in the territory; if you want one of the best claims in Oklahoma; if you want to get the best at little cost; if you want timber and water in abundance; if you want an ideal home in a law-abiding community, come to County G."[143]

The newspapers joined with the railroads in their efforts to attract settlers to their communities. The federal government had granted the railroads free land for their tracks, and railroad owners knew their own prosperity depended on the growth of population centers along their lines. As railroad workers laid train tracks across the great expanses of the West, company officials sent self-serving information to newspaper publishers and purchased advertising in hopes of enticing people westward. In addition, the railroads subsidized colonization companies to promote settlement along their lines. In the words of railroad magnate James J. Hill, the railroad "has opened up new territory, brought in population, created new industries and new wealth. It has served not as a mere connecting link between communities, but as a creative energy to bring them into existence."[144]

One theme within frontier journalism's discourse of boosterism was the promotion of social order. Many Americans believed the nation's remote frontier communities were filled with unruly and potentially dangerous people. To counteract this notion, newspaper editors published columns with messages designed to convince anyone considering making such locations home that they would be living among prosperous, respectable, law-abiding citizens. In 1851, the editor of the *Anthony Express* published this message about the kind of people needed in Minnesota Territory: "We want Farmers . . . Mechanics . . . Lawyers . . . Ministers . . . Physicians. . . . Last, though not least, *young ladies* are wanted."[145]

Immigrants from Europe and the British Isles were flooding the United States throughout the nineteenth century, and much of the material published to promote the settlement of the West was directed at them. Minnesota, which grew in population from 6,000 people in 1850 to 1.3 million in 1890, was especially attractive to German, Swedish, Norwegian, and Irish immigrants. The territory was opened for settlement in the early 1850s by the cession of large tracts of land to the federal government by the Ojibwe and Dakota Native American people. In 1862, the federal Homestead Act made free land available to all who wished to occupy it.

Newspapers such as the *Emigrant Aid Journal* were established in the frontier to promote the creation of communities that at the time only existed on paper. One of these towns was the dream of an eccentric genius named Ignatius Donnelly; it would be called Nininger. Donnelly selected a site for Nininger, which he envisioned as a utopian cooperative community on the Mississippi River, and even before moving to Minnesota from Philadelphia, he established the *Journal* in December 1856 with business partner Philip Rohr. The paper was printed on large sheets—twenty by twenty-six inches—and much of it was in German. The pages were decorated with images of waterfalls, steamboats, wagon trains, and railroad cars, and they included the words, rendered in large type: "'Dost thou know how to play the fiddle?' 'No,' answered Themistocles, 'but I understand the art of raising a little village into a great city.'" Donnelly's hopes for Nininger were not fulfilled. After a few people established an agrarian cooperative near a large house he built for himself, the real estate crash of 1857 put them all out of business.

In contrast to Donnelly, other promoters had better luck attracting immigrants to the communities they were hoping to build. Before 1790, most of America's foreign-born were from Africa. After the turn of the century, increasing numbers of immigrants came from continental European and Scandinavian countries, as well as from the British Isles. After 1820, the largest number of immigrants were from Germany, and many of them settled in the states and territories of the Midwest. German-language newspapers had been published in America since 1732, when Benjamin Franklin printed his first paper in Philadelphia, but as Germans flooded into the country in increasing numbers in the next century, these newspapers multiplied. During the century preceding World War I, a pluralistic German-language culture existed in America; as late as 1910, an estimated nine million people in the United States still regarded German as their mother tongue. They formed the readership of a large variety of German-language newspapers and other publications. One source estimates that at its zenith, the German-language press consisted of more than eight hundred daily and weekly newspapers and magazines.[146]

The desire to establish newspapers and magazines was strong among all ethnic groups whose members migrated to America. In fact, some newcomers found more papers printed in their language in the United States than in their homeland. At the turn of the nineteenth century, for example, there were six Yiddish dailies in New York City. Across the nineteenth and early twentieth centuries, America's foreign-language press flourished.

A spirited competition developed among those settling the frontier territories, and newspaper editors published essays and speeches that reflected the tone of these contests. In 1857, an address Ignatius Donnelly had given at the Broadway House in New York City was printed. In describing the topography of the Minnesota Territory, Donnelly had made the following comment on the bluffs of the Mississippi: "The land has spirit enough to get up a little, instead of lying stretched out in the Illinois fashion, as if laboring under a chronic fever and ague."[147]

Disputes often broke out in papers over which towns should win the battles over the location of county seats. One such disagreement erupted in 1887 between the Garfield County, Kansas, towns of Ravanna and Eminence. An editorial in the *County Call* asserted: "In the interest in humanity, common decency and honest government we desire that this enterprising, God fearing and progressive city of Ravanna shall be and remain the permanent county seat of this magnificent county, dowered by nature with a climate that makes the most favored part of Italy seem by comparison like a fever-breeding miasmatic swamp."[148] The situation became so volatile that the American West's famous gunfighter and lawman Bat Masterson and twenty deputies from Dodge City were hired to keep the peace during the first election in 1887, in which Ravanna won the honor by thirty-five votes. In response, the citizens of Eminence brought suit, alleging the ballot box had been stuffed. The Kansas Supreme Court agreed, and in 1889, the seat was transferred to Eminence. In 1892, the court decided Garfield County was illegally organized, having less than the 432 square miles required by the state constitution.[149]

Nineteenth-century Americans' desire for expansion was manifested not only in their use of newspapers for promotional purposes but also in their desire for speedier news. As people traveled across the Appalachian Mountains to start new lives in the West, the slowness of news delivery became ever more apparent. In addition, the wars the nation was involved in during the early decades of the century accentuated this problem. The century's first war, the Tripolitan War of 1801–1805, was fought in the Mediterranean Sea, thousands of miles away. It took weeks for ships from the Mediterranean to arrive with their batches of letters and reports on the war's progress. In comparison to the toll of later wars, Americans did not suffer a great number of casualties in this conflict, but the difficulties inherent in the acquisition of news from so far away fostered much frustration among those most directly affected by the war.

This sentiment would be felt again in the War of 1812 when it took weeks to receive news of battles and peace negotiations. Frustrations over slow communication reached the boiling point when the British burned Washington, D.C., on August 24, 1814. Residents of Philadelphia, for example, who were 126 miles away, would not receive news of the capitulation of the capital until twenty-four hours later. Following this, it would take a day longer for the news to reach New York City and a week for it to reach Raleigh, North Carolina. And though it was hailed as a great moral victory, the battle of New Orleans was, in fact, needlessly fought because news of a peace treaty, which had been signed in Europe, arrived too late.

After newspapers began utilizing the telegraph in the mid-1840s, anxiety over what was happening at the war front were replaced by the demand that news be available on all days of the week. During the Civil War, a ban on Sunday editions was lifted so the public could get newspapers every day of the week. In response, the operators of the country's papers recommitted themselves to their old race to be the fastest publishers. To establish reputations as such, some used carrier pigeons to fly news reports from distant points to eastern cities.

In 1835, the federal government displayed an interest in faster news delivery by establishing regular pony express service between Philadelphia and New York. A year later, travel time from New York to New Orleans had been cut to seven days. In 1841, a group of newspaper editors hired a special locomotive to carry President William Harrison's inaugural address from Washington to Baltimore, Philadelphia, and New York. The papers involved in this plan were able to scoop their competitors by twenty-four hours. Eventually, the steamship also speeded up the gathering of news, as travel across the Atlantic was reduced from weeks to days.

The telegraph gave those seeking speed in the transmission of news a tremendous boost. On May 24, 1844, Samuel Morse sat in the old Supreme Court chamber in Washington, D.C., and tapped out a message in code. Later that afternoon, he sent the first telegraphic message published in a newspaper to the *Baltimore Patriot:* "One o'clock—There has just been made a motion in the House to go into committee of the whole on the Oregon question. Rejected—ayes, 79; nays, 86." The significance of this report did not lie in the message itself but in what it promised for the future—a new system of communication whereby news could be sent instantly across vast distances without someone or something carrying it.

Americans were entranced by the possibility of instantaneous transmission of communications across the far reaches of the Republic. In a sermon to his Boston congregation, the Reverend Ezra Gannett said electricity was both "the swift-winged messenger of destruction" as well as the "vital energy of material creation."[150] Newspaper publishers were quick to make use of the new invention. In May 1846, President James K. Polk's message to Congress calling for war with Mexico was telegraphed to Baltimore for the exclusive use of that city's *Sun* newspaper.

Big-city newspapers were not the only ones whose readers benefited from the faster delivery of news via the telegraph. Printers in the West's small towns recognized that the telegraph would give them a boost in their efforts to serve their readers, who had been forced to wait for intolerably long periods of time for news from the East. The faster news delivery ushered in by the telegraph also led to the establishment of more newspapers. In Illinois, thirty papers were founded during the decade following the start of telegraphic news service.

The arrival of the first telegraphed news in towns along the lines extending out from the nation's eastern population centers was exciting. When the telegraph wire from Albany reached Utica, New York, in early 1846, the town's *Daily Gazette* received its first telegraphic bulletins. The news was so fresh and the transmission so novel that the editor devoted a column to the dispatches. By March, the publishers at Utica and other upstate papers had organized what became the New York State Associated Press. Nineteen papers had joined the first U.S. news service by August, and news agents were employed in Albany and New York City. A telegraph line linked Albany and Buffalo by July and Albany and New York City in September.[151]

The Associated Press, today the world's largest cooperative news-gathering agency, was founded under a different name in New York City two years after Morse unveiled his telegraph. The organization did not become known as the AP until 1860. The idea behind the venture was for the papers to pool their resources to improve their coverage of the Mexican-American War. The five New York papers that joined in the agreement were the *Sun,* the *Journal of Commerce,* the *Courier and Enquirer,* the *Herald,* and the *Express.* The group's members invested not only in the telegraph but also in a combination of services designed to speed up and reduce the cost of news delivery. In 1849, the Associated Press opened the first bureau outside the United States, in Halifax, Nova Scotia, to meet ships from Europe before they docked in New York.

Americans' preoccupation with politics and government in the early years of the nation helps explain the increasing numbers of newspapers established in the decades following the American

Revolution. The emergence of the country's earliest political parties was an important part of this process. By the presidential election of 1801, both the fledgling Federalist and Jeffersonian Republican Parties had established their own newspapers. Thomas Jefferson's party was ably represented by the *National Intelligencer,* one of the papers established in 1800 at Washington, D.C. Rivaling the *Intelligencer* were popular Federalist papers such as the *Washington Federalist,* Boston's *Columbian Centinel,* New York's *Evening Post,* Baltimore's *Federal Republican,* and a host of others whose publishers capitalized on and contributed to the contentious and acrimonious debates over the era's many pressing political and constitutional questions.

Reports on proceedings of governmental bodies and reproductions of legislative bills and other documents filled the columns of newspapers whose publishers were awarded government contracts to print such materials. Those not awarded such lucrative government patronage were at a disadvantage, but they nevertheless often published information about government proceedings to please their customers, who were hungry for such news.

In addition to their interest in politics, Americans enjoyed the newspapers for all the extras they provided as well. A little piece circulated in papers across the early decades of the century explained what the day's publications had to offer: "A NEWS-PAPER is a bill of fare, containing a variety of dishes, suited to the different tastes and appetites of those who sit down at the entertainment. Politics are *beef steaks.* . . . Essays, humorous, speculative, moral and divine, are a *fine boiled dish.* . . . Ship news is a *glass of grog at 'leven*—Poetry is *custard*—Marriages are *sweetmeats*—Ballads and love-ditties, *plum puddings* . . . and epigrams, are *seasoning spice* and *mustard.*"[152]

Over the course of the nineteenth century, Americans developed a stronger interest than existed before the American Revolution in reading local news in their papers. The country's earliest newspapers published more news about far-away places than they did about what was happening right at home. Before the American Revolution, royal authorities discouraged the publication of local information, and people in general did not have much tolerance for controversy. Much of what appeared in early papers was copied from other newspapers or sent in by correspondents from afar.

While early newspapers generally included a modicum of local news, routines for the systematic gathering and dissemination of this news did not become commonplace until the operators of New York City's penny papers began developing them in the 1830s. British penny papers had employed people to go to local courts to learn about crime since the early 1820s, but American editors were not inclined to adopt the practice. However, as he prepared to publish the premier issue of the America's first penny paper, the *New York Sun,* Benjamin H. Day hired Londoner George W. Wisner to report from the New York City Police Court. The first issue of the *Sun,* published on September 3, 1883, carried this report: "John McMan, brought up for whipping Juda McMan, his darling wife—excuse was, that his head was rather thick, in consequence of taking a wee drop of whiskey. Not being able to find bail, he was accommodated with a room in Bridewell [the city jail]."

The idea of developing networks of reporters who would canvas nearby neighborhoods, government-sponsored offices, and private businesses for news took off during the 1830s, and by the end of the century, the role of the local news reporter was firmly entrenched both in city papers and in small-town establishments as well. In 1862, Samuel Clemens, who had not yet assumed the pen name Mark Twain, was hired as a reporter by the owners of the *Territorial Enterprise,* at Virginia City, Nevada. As he recalled later in *Roughing It,* Clemens would be paid $25 per week "to go all over town and ask all sorts of people all sorts of questions, make notes of the information gained, and write them out for publication." When he became city editor, he described the responsibilities of his paper: "Our duty is to keep the universe thoroughly posted concerning murders and street fights, and balls, and theaters, and pack-trains, and churches, and lectures, and school-houses, and city military affairs, and highway robberies, and Bible societies, and hay-wagons, and a thousand other things which it is in the province of local reporters to keep track of and magnify into undue importance for the instruction of the readers of this great daily newspaper."[153]

A common practice on small-town newspapers was to establish teams of neighborhood reporters, although they were called correspondents and did not earn much, if anything, from their part-time endeavors. Nevertheless, the role played by these correspondents helped readers who wanted to read what was going on across their neighborhoods. When George H. Hand started a newspaper called the *Settler,* in Ludell, Kansas, on October 18, 1884, he stressed the importance of neighborhood news in his first issue's salutatory statement. He wrote: "When a country editor realizes the fact that he doesn't know it all, and accords merit where it belongs, correspondents will step to the front and assist in making a paper. We are even now looking, and probably won't be compelled to look long, for assistance with more brains than we possess."[154]

Part of the nineteenth-century citizens' thirst for more and more news originated in their growing interest in a broadening range of social and cultural agendas. In 1800, two categories of newspapers predominated in America: those that catered to the members of their communities' mercantile establishments and those published mainly in the interests of individuals in political power, that is, a community's prosperous white men. Overlooked by most newspapers were the concerns of the nation's women, laborers, poor, African Americans, Native Americans, and radicals, among others. But things changed dramatically over the next century, and by 1900, it must have seemed to Americans as though a newspaper was published for every imaginable group.

In the years leading up to the Civil War, American newspaper editors ignored African Americans in the columns of their papers unless they had run away from their owners or were involved in a slave rebellion. Slavery had led to periodic acts of violent resistance throughout the centuries it was permitted in America. Historian Herbert Aptheker found documentary evidence of more than 250 revolts and conspiracies involving ten or more slaves in American history.[155] Authorities in communities close to the rebellion often prohibited newspapers from printing accounts of uprisings, since they believed such stories would lead to further violence. But reports and comments about slave rebellions did occasionally make it into these papers, and many more were published in places far away from where the incidents occurred. In 1800, a brief extract from a letter was published in the *Virginia Herald,* in the town of Fredericksburg, after a slave insurrection took place in nearby Richmond. Blaming an overly permissive society for the event, the writer of the letter chided the Richmond press for failing to publish details related to the rebellion. Sixteen years later, a letter writer from Camden, South Carolina, sent around a report titled "A South Carolina Plot." As it appeared in the *New-York Evening Post,* it started: "Our gaol is filled with negroes. They are stretched on their backs on the bare floor, and scarcely move their heads; but have a strong guard placed over them. . . . This is really a dreadful situation to be in—I think it is time for us to leave a country where we cannot go to bed in safety."[156]

In a similar vein, while early-nineteenth-century newspapers did publish some reports and commentary about Native Americans, such coverage was generally not extensive anywhere but in the West. In addition, wherever news of Native American people was published, it was generally unsympathetic in nature. The period leading up to and immediately following the famous battle of Tippecanoe, which took place in western Indiana on November 7 and 8 in 1811, is an interesting case in point. At daybreak on November 7, a band of Shawnee warriors and 1,000 American soldiers met in battle. The Shawnees were led by a man called the Prophet, the brother of famous Shawnee tribal leader Tecumseh, and U.S. troops were led by General William Henry Harrison. Two hours later, 37 American soldiers were dead (25 would later die of injuries), and more than 126 were wounded. The Indians' casualties are unknown, but their spirit was crushed.

The battle's background goes back at least to the American Revolution, when native people were increasingly pushed out of their ancestral homes as white Americans moved west. Native Americans were divided as to how to respond to the policies of the U.S. government, which focused on "civilizing" them and placating them with treaties. Alliances between native groups that had been attempted over the years had largely ended in failure. But when Tecumseh started traveling through America in hopes of organizing a confederacy of all Indian people, U.S. leaders were alarmed. Some historians see the defeat of the Shawnee at Tippecanoe as the quashing of the Indian people's last hope in their struggle to maintain the ways of their ancestors.

Through the weeks and months leading up to the battle, reports on the movements of Tecumseh, the Prophet, and their associates grew more common, as editors became eager to publish anything they could about the increasingly ominous signs that hostilities were looming. Some of these reports were reprinted in eastern seaboard papers, especially those that focused on a possible link between Native Americans and the British. Tensions in the East over the possibility of war with Great Britain were high, and those in favor of war capitalized on the news of a possible pact between the Indians and the British.

Concerns about the poor treatment of various groups of Americans, such as slaves and Native Americans, eventually culminated in a full-blown social movement. Sometimes called the first reform era, its origins lay in a matrix of unrest and intellectual ferment in which both liberals and conservatives addressed a broad array of social ills. Early indicators of the movement were visible in the late 1820s, when newspapers began appearing to serve the interests of abolitionists, labor organizations, Native Americans, and African Americans. While these papers often consisted largely of editorial commentary, their editors included sizable amounts of news in their columns as well.

Samuel Cornish and John B. Russwurm established America's first African American newspaper, *Freedom's Journal,* in 1827 in New York City. The men wanted to protest the goals of an organization called the American Colonization Society. Although the society's leaders were opposed to slavery, their solution was to send freed slaves, along with free blacks, back to Africa to establish their own colonies. When the city's editors told Cornish and Russwurm that their statements of protest against the society would not be published, the two men decided to establish their own newspaper. They wrote: "We wish to plead our own cause

. . . [because for] too long others have spoken for us. Too long has the public been deceived by misrepresentations."[157]

A friend of Cornish's, reformer Theodore Wright, later recalled *Freedom's Journal* "came like a clap of thunder" at a time when free black opponents to colonization despaired of ever making themselves heard. African Americans founded some forty papers before 1865 and responded to the end of slavery by starting more than a thousand by 1900.

The mainstream press's failure to promote the causes of abolitionists seeking to eliminate the nation's system of slavery led to the establishment of antislavery newspapers. The first of these was the *Liberator,* which was started by William Lloyd Garrison in 1831. Funded and largely owned by whites, this press served an important networking function for the antislavery movement. Using new technologies, the Anti-slavery Society flooded the mails in 1835 with literature, thereby inflating its power and influence.

Only a few publishers of general-purpose newspapers were willing to campaign against slavery, and those who did were generally citizens of the Free States. The editors of a number of newspapers contributed to the cause of abolitionism by publishing letters from former citizens who had moved west to spread the word against slavery. One of these correspondents was Julia Lovejoy, who moved with her minister husband, Charles, to the town of Manhattan on the Kansas frontier in 1855. A series of letters she sent east told of life on the prairie but also discussed abolitionism and the climate of violence that surrounded the question of whether Kansas would become a free or slave state. Her letters were printed in the *Independent Democrat* in Concord, New Hampshire; the *Granite State Whig* in Lebanon, New Hampshire; the *New York Tribune*; the *Zion's Herald* in Boston; the *Central Christian Advocate* in St. Louis; and the *Christian Messenger* in Montpelier, Vermont.

One southern newspaper publisher who risked everything when he decided to use his printing press to distribute abolitionist materials was William Swaim, who edited North Carolina's *Greensborough Patriot* from 1829 to 1835. In the spring of 1829, Swaim started using the columns of his newspaper to support abolitionism and several other social, educational, and political reform movements. In 1830, he wrote and printed a pamphlet titled *Address to the People of North Carolina on the Evils of Slavery.* In response, his state's General Assembly published a resolution against him for publishing "seditious and libelous" literature.

Since most American newspaper editors were unsympathetic to the concerns of the country's Native American people, these people decided to start publishing their own papers. In 1828, the *Cherokee Phoenix* became America's first Native American newspaper. Printed in New Echota, Georgia, the paper was established to interfere with the federal government's Indian policies, which were increasingly based on a system of removal. The *Cherokee Phoenix* was published weekly until May 1834, when the Cherokee annuity was not paid and the presses came to a stop. In the decades that followed, dozens of additional newspapers were founded, edited, or maintained by American Indians. While their publishers always had to struggle financially, the papers served their communities in ways the regular papers did not.[158]

America's first newspapers published to further the interests of the working class appeared in the late 1820s after the depression of the winter of 1828–1829 and the rising cost of living led to hard times. The first labor newspaper, the *Journeyman Mechanic's Advocate,* was started in Philadelphia in 1827. The paper only lasted a year, but a successor, the *Mechanic's Free Press,* was able to maintain a healthy circulation of around fifteen hundred until the detrimental effects of the panic of 1837 killed it.

The nation's first national labor organization, the National Trades Union, was founded in 1834. A strong supporter of the union was the *Working Man's Advocate,* which was founded in New York City in 1829 by George H. Evans. Another supporter of the labor movement was Frances "Fanny" Wright, the publisher of a paper called the *Free Enquirer.* In addition, Wright's newspaper became important in the New Harmony, Indiana, utopian experiment conducted by Robert Dale Owen.

In the mid-1850s, a group of German immigrants brought Marxian socialism to America. Once in the United States, they became active in the German American labor movement and bombarded Americans with calls to end capitalism through organized activity. Outstanding among these early disseminators of Marxism was Joseph Weydemeyer, who, as a newspaper editor and union organizer, worked not only to strengthen American trade unionism but also to educate union members on the importance of political action. In 1852, Weydemeyer held that "there should be no division between economics and politics."[159] Like those who ran the period's labor papers, many operators of socialist newspapers found it difficult to sustain their publications financially. One radical paper that did break through to a mass audience was the *Appeal to Reason,* which was published in Girard, Kansas. This weekly had a circulation of more than six hundred thousand in 1912, and an "appeal army" of eighty thousand subscription agents was busy in every state. Its publisher, Julius A. Wayland, intended his paper to help the Socialist Party appeal to those not yet convinced of the wisdom of its ideology.

Amelia Jenks Bloomer started America's first prominent woman's rights newspaper, the *Lily,* in 1849 in Seneca Falls, New York. Her goal was to help women campaign against the consumption of alcohol. In describing her feelings about the newspaper, she said: "It was a needed instrument to spread abroad the truth of a new gospel to woman, and I could not withhold my hand to stay the work I had begun. I saw not the end from the beginning and dreamed where to my propositions to society would lead me."[160]

Bloomer's newspaper was the first in a long series of papers established during the nineteenth and early twentieth centuries to support both the temperance and the suffrage movements. Temperance efforts existed in antiquity, but the movement really came into its own as a reaction to the pervasive use of distilled beverages in modern times. In the early 1800s, pledges of abstinence were promulgated by preachers such as John Bartholomew Gough. Some of America's earliest temperance associations were established in New York in 1808 and in Massachusetts in 1813. By the 1830s, local temperance groups had been organized in thousands of towns across the country.

Although the first women's convention, held in Seneca Falls, New York, in 1848, is usually considered the beginning of the suffrage movement, its origins in the United States were in the earlier temperance and abolitionist campaigns. Well-known suffrage leaders, such as Angelina and Sarah Grimke, Lydia Child, Lucy Stone, Elizabeth Cady Stanton, and Susan B. Anthony, for example, became involved in woman's suffrage via the antislavery movement. Stanton and Anthony established a newspaper devoted to suffrage and other causes, called the *Revolution,* in 1868. Three years later, Abigail Scott Duniway started *New Northwest,* a weekly newspaper that focused on women's rights and suffrage.

Throughout the nineteenth and early twentieth centuries, the period often labeled as the golden age of the newspaper, an array of new technologies adopted by publishers helped them bring more and different news, more quickly, to Americans. Improvements in printing technologies, such as the web-fed rotary press, typesetting machines, and steam-powered and eventually electricity-powered presses, among many others, all had an effect on the news. But technologies alone are not accountable for the changes in news. Because of myriad social developments, evolving cultural values, economic events and trends, human tragedies such as wars and disasters, and a host of other contextual factors, the news has been continuously reinvented.

———————————◇———————————

FIVE

PRINTERS AND READERS

Technologies are human creations, and history is so full of stories of their inventions that most of us know who invented the steam engine, automobile, and other important developments. But who invented the technologies of journalism? The simplest answer is Johannes Gutenberg, Samuel F. B. Morse, Guglielmo Marconi, and the others involved in their initial creations. But the stories of the inventions of journalism's technologies go beyond this handful of famous people. The printing press, radio, and camera would not have become associated with journalism without human agency, that is, without the collective efforts of two additional groups of people—the printers, radio operators, and photographers who used them to produce news and the readers, listeners, and other members of the public who became consumers of the news in all its myriad forms.

Printers, publishers, and groups of news readers, viewers, and audiences did not exist in America when it was populated largely by indigenous people and English and European immigrants who lived in the wilderness or a few scattered population centers along

the eastern seaboard. Ships and rudimentary mail systems circulated news in the form of letters and other handwritten materials.
Printed newspapers were imported from continental Europe and
England, but most news was disseminated largely through conversation, decree, and religious sermons.

The arrival of printing in the colonies in 1638 initially did little
to change such news practices. While some news was published in
printed proclamations, broadsides, and pamphlets after the arrival
of the first provincial printing press at Cambridge, sparse popula-
tions and a general lack of commercial enterprise in the earliest
British American communities discouraged the emergence of locally produced papers. In addition, England's strict regulation of
printing presses, which commenced in the 1660s, was a serious de-
terrent to anyone thinking of starting a newspaper.

During the late seventeenth and early eighteenth centuries, an
environment more attractive to printers and others with notions
about starting papers developed. Many of colonial America's earliest printers and editors came from Great Britain, where papers
had been published for generations. Up to the middle of the eighteenth century, America's newspaper business was more like a
branch of the English publishing system than a separate entity with
its own character. Over time, however, the printers and editors
used the printing press to help create a community with values that
were increasingly American.

Colonial America's first newspaper publisher, Benjamin Harris,
learned the printing trade in his home country of England. After
arriving in America to escape a jail sentence for publishing an in-
cendiary account of a supposed papist plot against England, Harris
cobbled together a plan to make a living. Part of his agenda involved the publication of a newspaper, and in Boston on September 25, 1690, he issued *Publick Occurrences, Both Forreign and Dome-*

stick. The paper included commentary that immediately alarmed the British authorities. Not only did Harris's paper refer to an attack on some Indians who had fought with the English against the French but it also alluded to a salacious rumor about the king of France. The authorities quashed the paper before Harris could issue any additional numbers. They pronounced that *Publick Occurrences* was "a pamphlet published contrary to law and containing reflections of a very high nature."[161]

Fourteen years later, on April 24, 1704, America's second newspaper, the *Boston News-Letter,* was started. The paper was published and edited under the auspices of John Campbell, the city's postmaster. Campbell was an Anglican conservative who emigrated to Boston from Scotland in the 1690s. After befriending members of the town's leadership, he was appointed constable in 1699 and postmaster a few years later. As postmaster, Campbell had access to news and information and had franking privileges that put him in an excellent position to issue a newspaper. After issuing the *News-Letter* in handwritten form, he decided his enterprise might be more lucrative if he hired a printer and advertising solicitor. Unskilled in the art of printing, Campbell worked out an arrangement with Bartholomew Green to print the paper.

Censorship was not an issue for Campbell, whose legal status as postmaster gave him license to publish the *News-Letter.* Because he had no intention of putting anything in the paper that would offend the authorities, his paper came out on a regular basis with no interference from the local officials. The one-page publication typically contained foreign news copied from London newspapers and local items concerning shipping, sermons, deaths, accidents, fires, and political appointments. Campbell published the *News-Letter* until 1722, when he sold it to its printer, Green. It was continued under a succession of printers and editors until 1776, when the British evacuated Boston at the start of the American Revolution.

From such a modest beginning, an emerging group of printers and editors shaped the role of the printing press as conveyor of news and editorial opinion. Thirty-one of the forty Bostonians who became involved in newspaper projects during the period 1696 to 1775 were printers, seven were postmasters, and two came from the ranks of the city's legal, publishing, and bookselling communities. A typical newspaper printer or editor was involved in a variety of publishing and printing projects. In addition to newspapers, items that appeared under their imprimaturs included books, pamphlets, almanacs, tracts, and any other materials that might attract readers.

Getting out a paper was a labor-intensive process, and printers generally acquired indentured apprentices to help with their more onerous tasks. But along with physical strength and stamina, printing required skills in spelling, composition, and occasionally writing. Although printers often downplayed the intellectual components of printing by referring to themselves as "meer mechanics," they demonstrated their proficiency with words every time they put out a paper. After taking over the *Pennsylvania Gazette* in 1729, Benjamin Franklin wrote about the skills needed to publish a good paper:

> To publish a good News-Paper is not so easy an Undertaking as many People imagine it to be. The Author of the Gazette (in the Opinion of the Learned) ought to be qualified with an extensive Acquaintance with Languages, a great Easiness and Command of Writing and Relating things cleanly and intelligibly, and in a few Words; he should be able to speak of War both by Land and Sea; be well acquainted with Geography, with the History of the

time, with the several Interests of Princes and States, the Secrets of Courts, and the manners and Customs of all Nations. Men thus accomplish'd are very rare in this remote Part of the World; and it would be well if the Writer of these Papers could make up among his Friends what is wanting in himself.[162]

Franklin stands out in early America as its most famous newspaper printer. Born at Boston in 1706, two years after Campbell established the *Boston News-Letter,* he was apprenticed as a boy to his older brother, James Franklin, the operator of a print shop. In 1721, the older Franklin started a newspaper titled the *New-England Courant.* Benjamin was turned down when he asked his brother if he could write for the paper. Undaunted, he began sliding a series of letters he wrote under the door of the print shop. Benjamin's pseudonym was Silence Dogood, a fictional widow with many complaints about the world, especially in relation to how women were treated. After the letters were published and began to draw a lot of attention, Benjamin confessed his deeds to his brother, who became very exasperated. According to some accounts, Benjamin was harangued and even beaten by his older brother during the years of his apprenticeship.

The Franklins would soon become embroiled in a dispute over whether inoculation against smallpox made people sick or helped them become immune to the scourge that attacked and killed so many people in that era of history. James Franklin took a position against inoculation, in opposition to a number of well-known authorities, including the esteemed Rev. Cotton Mather. Although many Bostonians agreed with him, they did not like the way he made fun of the clergy in the columns of his paper. After he was jailed for his offenses, James assigned Benjamin the task of bringing out the paper. Yet instead of being grateful to his younger brother when he got out of jail, James continued to treat him with disdain.

In 1723, when Benjamin finally decided he had taken enough from his brother, he left Boston to start a life of his own. He ended up at Philadelphia, where he was able to find work again as an apprentice. In 1726, at age twenty, Franklin developed a "plan" for regulating his future conduct. In part, his motivation stemmed from Philippians 4:8, which reads: "Finally, brothers, whatever is true, whatever is noble, whatever is right, whatever is pure, whatever is lovely, whatever is admirable—if anything is excellent or praiseworthy—think about such things." Franklin's sixth rule, which was devoted to the spirit of "Industry," required that he "Lose no time. Be always employed in something useful. Cut off all unnecessary actions."[163]

In 1729, after years of working for others, he and his wife, Deborah, purchased their own newspaper, the *Pennsylvania Gazette*. The *Gazette* quickly became the most successful newspaper in the colonies. Franklin was driven by a spirit of industriousness and competition that has been a hallmark of American journalism since the middle of the eighteenth century. Competition between journalists has led many to strive for the speediest and most efficient technologies available. It also helps explain developments in news and the news industry that are unconnected to technology.

John Peter Zenger was another newspaper printer who became famous in the history of newspaper journalism. A Germany immigrant, Zenger arrived in America in 1710. On reaching a suitable age, he was indentured to New York City's only printer, William Bradford. In 1726, Zenger established his own print shop, and in 1733, he was approached by a group of wealthy New Yorkers who asked him if he would serve as the printer of a newspaper they were starting, the *New-York Gazette*. He agreed and ended up in jail and on trial for seditious libel because of what he printed. The paper's owners had become deeply embroiled in a campaign against the royal governor, William Crosby. Although it was generally assumed that Zenger would lose in court, the jury came back with a not guilty verdict because the material published was based on fact. In previous libel courts, publishing fact had always led to a conviction. The verdict was received with elation among those who had turned against the royal authorities. After his release from jail, Zenger printed a verbatim account of the trial.

Although most of the early Americans who operated printing presses to circulate news did not become as widely known as Franklin and Zenger, over time they forged a collective identity that linked them to the printing press. Few came from the ranks of colonial society's politically elite groups, but the diversity of the pursuits of the colonial printers helped elevate them to a level neither as low as "meer mechanics" nor as high as society "principals." Motivated by keen entrepreneurial ambitions, many printers would do whatever it took to keep their publishing businesses on solid financial ground. Some operated bookstores and job-printing businesses; others entered into the mercantile field. A few served in appointed local governmental or quasi-governmental offices. The multiplicity of a printer's activities meant he could become "much more" because "by the sum of his activities, a printer might well become a prominent man—unavoidably involved in a wide range of local affairs, though not necessarily with effective influence."[164]

Despite the efforts of printers to elevate their status in society, the newspaper business grew slowly during the decades leading up to the American Revolution. From 1704 to the Revolution, a total of thirty-seven newspapers were issued in the colonies. John Campbell had the newspaper field to himself until 1719, when William Brooker replaced him as postmaster. When Campbell refused to give up the *News-Letter,* Brooker started the colony's second regularly published newspaper, the *Boston Gazette.* Not until after the Revolution would the growth of the newspaper business gather any discernible momentum.

The Revolution was among the first major events in American history in which the operators of printing presses would collectively interject themselves into the public sphere. After James Franklin and John Peter Zenger won their battles against local authorities, strictures against the operators of printing presses were relaxed for a time. But the atmosphere heated up once again when the British government passed the 1765 Stamp Act, the symbolic beginning of the American Revolutionary War period. As British America divided over the question of whether the colonies should throw off the yoke of British rule, printers and editors were increasingly drawn into the fray. From 1765 to the start of war, arguments were seen in the newspapers over the Stamp Act, the call for "No taxation without representation," the Nonimportation Agreements, the Boston Massacre, the Tea Act and the Boston Tea Party, and ultimately the question of whether to separate from England. Over the years of the Revolution, three Boston printers—Benjamin Edes, John Gill, and Isaiah Thomas—never failed to rail against the British in the pages of their newspapers.

In the summer of 1765, Edes joined the group that eventually became known as the Sons of Liberty. Aware that his printing press would be useful to the cause, he and his fellow printer John Gill filled their paper, the *Boston Gazette,* with attacks against the tax and England. Although the Stamp Act was repealed in 1766, the British subsequently imposed further taxes on the Americans. In 1770, violence erupted in Boston when the British retaliated against an American mob by killing five citizens. By 1776, when the Declaration of Independence was issued and Thomas Paine announced that "these are the times that try men's souls" in *The Crisis,* two groups within America's community of printers had coalesced—those called patriots and a group called loyalist printers. Throughout the war, these printers fought propaganda battles alongside those who served in the military. The situation was dangerous for both sides through the years of the war. Four Boston printers on the side of the British—Margaret Draper, John Howe, John Hicks, and Nathaniel Mills—were compelled to leave the city when the British evacuated in 1776. At the war's conclusion, most loyalist printers left America, eventually making their way to Canada.

By the time of the 1783 peace treaty, the number of newspapers published in America had decreased from nearly forty to about twenty. Although small in number, however, printers in the post-Revolution era enjoyed a period of enhanced status. Compared to the pressure they experienced before the Revolution to downplay any political strife they observed in their communities, they now had a heightened sense of power. In 1793, publishers Alexander Young and Samuel Etheridge commented at length about the newfound legitimacy of the newspaper in a statement issued during their establishment of the *Massachusetts Mercury.* They wrote:

> At no period, since the discovery of printing, has there ever been so interesting an era as the present. . . . And while the historian is . . . employed to delineate her progress in Arms and Arts, the Printer of a weekly Paper, if faithful to his trust, furnishes in the minutiae of successive detail, events less splendid than those which adorn the historic page, but vastly more interesting to the present actors in the theater of existence. Newpapers originally fanned that favored flame of Liberty, which first was kindled on

the Columbian Altar, and from thence with unexampled rapidity has spread to the furthest bourne [*sic*] of Europe, illuminating the universe of Man in its progress, and giving freedom to myriads of lives.[165]

Although the war had taken a toll on the country's newspapers, their numbers had increased to several hundred by 1800. American printers suffered a brief setback through the Federalist government's imposition of the 1798 Alien and Sedition Acts. But after the laws expired in 1801, printers and editors eventually gained recognition as society's legitimate providers of news and editorial opinion.

Along the way, newspaper printers helped elevate their status through self-serving communications distributed in print and though other channels. Newspaper prospectuses serve as a good example. Every publisher seeking to establish a new paper printed a prospectus filled not only with information about the proposed publication but also with messages designed to enhance the publisher's own reputation. As he established a newspaper in 1822 in Charleston, South Carolina, Edmund Morford reported in a prospectus to the town's citizens that he could be trusted to uphold their interests. He wrote: "The direction and management of the press is an undertaking of high responsibility. . . . As public patronage and favour are the sole support of a Gazette, the community has a right to exact of its publisher all the advantages that are to be expected, from his assumption of the character of one acting as the dispenser of intelligence. . . . That confidence . . . holds him by solemn ties, as pledged to consecrate it to the public good, to make it subservient to the prosperity and happiness of the country."[166]

In addition to newspaper prospectuses, journalists issued self-congratulatory messages in printed autobiographies, obituaries, masthead slogans, poems, and essays. A poem published in an 1802 issue of the *Salem (Mass.) Register* provided readers with information on the role and relationships of the paper's publisher: "Here shall the press the people's rights maintain, / Unaw'd by influence and unbrib'd by gain; / Here patriot truth its glorious precepts draw, / Pledg'd to religion, liberty and law."[167]

Another avenue used by journalists to promote their position in society, along with that of their newspapers, was the speaking engagement. Nineteenth-century newspaper editors were asked to speak at local events, such as Fourth of July picnics, and preside over public ceremonies, such as the openings of new buildings. The individuals of this small but influential group became well known as orators and members of the various lecture circuits that flourished in America at the time.

The role of the reader in the evolution of news and the granting of jurisdiction over its dissemination in the United States is also key in any study of the impact technology has had on the field. But compared to what we know about the printers and editors within America's burgeoning news community, we know little about newspaper readers. It is impossible, for example, to point to a particular individual known as the eighteenth century's quintessential newspaper patron. Nevertheless, people who read newspapers during this early period should be considered just as important in the transformation of the printing presses into a technology of journalism as the printers and editors who operated them.

Historians have often described the readers of America's early papers as members of society's educated and wealthy class with a growing taste for the news. Colonial America's printers and editors recognized this and attempted to use the knowledge to their advantage. Printer James Parker wrote in 1750 that Americans "can't be without" the news, a cultural predilection that he stated foreigners could not understand. Those who could not afford to buy newspapers, which were very expensive, went to their local taverns and coffeehouses to read and discuss the contents of the latest editions. The keepers of these establishments knew the members of their communities would keep coming for the materials they kept in their "reading rooms," as well as for the coffee and ale.

Further evidence of the public's interest in receiving the news in printed form is visible in statements published by newspaper printers and editors seeking to establish new publications. In his first issue of the *Boston Gazette* on December 21, 1719, William Brooker wrote: "The publishing of this Paper has been in compliance with the desires of several of the Merchants and others of this Town, as also at the repeated Instances of those People that live remote from hence, who have been prevented from having the News Paper sent them by the Post, ever since Mr. Campbell was removed from being Post-Master."

Likewise, on October 1, 1728, Samuel Keimer told the readers of his new newspaper, the *Pennsylvania Gazette, or Universal Instructor,* that he had been encouraged by "several Gentlemen in this, and the Neighbouring Provinces . . . to publish a Paper of Intelligence."

From the earliest newspapers through the American Revolution, readers told printers what they wanted to see in the papers, and the printers addressed such interests whenever possible. The papers carried a good amount of news about foreign affairs, politics, and government. In addition, they included information on local events, science, medicine, agriculture, literature, inventions, education, and social and cultural matters. From time to time, the papers covered such topics as money, Native Americans, woman's rights, the Great Awakening, religious divisions, and the lotteries. In 1735, for example, the May 19 issue of the *New-York Weekly Journal* published the statement of an anonymous writer who asserted that women ought to receive the same educations as men. Song lyrics and poetry were also published in the papers.

In the area of religion, a popular topic was the Great Awakening, one of history's most famous religious revivals. The best known of the movement's leaders was George Whitefield, whose preaching style drew thousands. In 1739, a poem extolling Whitefield's oratory virtues was published in the November 26, 1739, *New-York Weekly Journal*. Its author began with the words "WHITEFIELD! That Great, that pleasing Name."

Printers and editors of early American papers knew that news and commentary on politics and foreign affairs rarely failed to capture their readers' attention. From 1754 to 1760, colonists' desire for news was well served by a wealth of information in the papers related to the conflict between England and France over who would control North America. When the two countries declared war on each other in 1756, newspaper publisher Daniel Fowle discussed the colonists' need for news. In the first issue of the *New Hampshire Gazette,* on October 7, 1756, after telling his readers he had been urged by local people to start a new paper, he wrote:

> Every Lover of Mankind must feel a strong Desire to know what passes in the World, as well as within his own private Sphere; and particularly to be acquainted with the Affairs of his own Nation and Country—Especially at such a Time as this, when the British Nation is engaged in a just and necessary War with a powerful Enemy, the French, a War in which these American Colonists are most nearly interested, the Event of which must be of the utmost Importance both to us and all the British Dominians, every

true Englishman must be anxious to know from Time to Time the State of our Affairs at Home and in the Colonies.

On behalf of their readers, the operators of Americans' newspapers took very seriously the threat posed by the conflict between France and England. In 1756, a writer using the name "Virginia Centinel" put out an impassioned cry for vigilance that was reprinted across the colonies:

> Friends! Countrymen! . . . Awake! Arise! . . . When our Country, and all that is included in that important Word, is in most threatening Danger; when our Enemies are busy and unwearied in planning and executing their Schemes of Encroachments and Barbarity . . . when in short our All is at Stake . . . the Patriot Passions must be roused in every Breast capable of such generous Sensations. . . . Countrymen! Fellow-Subjects! Fellow-Protestants! to engage your Attention, I need only repeat, Your Country is in Danger.[168]

Early Americans' appreciation for journalism was reflected in the willingness of literate people to send letters and pieces of commentary for inclusion in the newspapers. Such correspondents were greatly depended on by editors, who could not easily go out and gather much news by themselves. Some of these writers preferred to remain anonymous and would send in their pieces unsigned or under pseudonyms. One of American journalism's most famous series of unsigned letters came out in 1767 and 1768. The first letter was published on December 21, 1767, in the *Boston Chronicle,* and by the time the remaining thirteen were published, they had been reprinted in newspapers across the colonies. The letters were written under the heading "Letters from a Pennsylvania Farmer," and the author's identity was widely known among the paper's readers. While he didn't sign his letters, John Dickinson did not disguise himself as a person seeking to unify colonial support against the British.

In addition to writing for the papers, colonists used the newspapers to post notices of a diverse nature. Merchants purchased space to advertise their goods. Members of the medical and legal communities publicized their services. Items on the arrivals and departures of ships were common in towns along the eastern seaboard. Private individuals used the paper to publish notices of runaway wives and slaves, goods that had been stolen, and the sale of lands and other property. Although it is difficult to assess with certainty the amount of support such advertisements provided to the printers, it is certain that in the eighteenth-century, they depended on advertising as one of their chief sources of revenue.

Publication figures for the period were low, especially when compared to circulation a century later, yet the demand for news led to increases in subscriptions over the course of the eighteenth century. Colonial America's newspapers were expensive, and the fact that anyone, even a wealthy person, was willing to pay the cost of an annual subscription suggests how highly news was valued. A year's subscription to the earliest colonial newspapers cost about $1.54, a figure representing about 11 percent of the average person's annual salary.[169] Circulation nonetheless gradually increased. In 1750, newspaper circulation averaged 600 copies per week. Fifteen years later, having received a boost from the Stamp Act crisis, circulations had grown as high as 1500 copies per week in some places, and by the time of the Revolution, it was up to 3500.

Circulations would not leap significantly higher until a group of urban publishers began selling their papers for a penny—five cents less than most of their competitors. According to the consumer price index in today's economy, a comparable change in price would drop the cost of a newspaper from $1.42 to $.24. By 1836, the *New York Sun* claimed to have a circulation greater than its eleven six-penny competitors combined.[170] Part of the success of these papers was attributable to their publishers' efforts to appeal to the Americans they claimed conventional papers had ignored—the masses—as opposed to the country's more elite groups.

In sum, during the press's first two centuries in America, human agency played an major part in the establishment of the printing press as a technology of journalism. Together, printers, editors, and news readers helped give the printing press a new purpose and meaning—that of an important journalistic agent. While the field of newspaper journalism was still a modest one in the period immediately following the American Revolution, a foundation had been laid for the future, and the newspaper would start to grow in the early decades of the next century. Through the nineteenth and twentieth centuries, human agency continued to serve a crucial role in the continuing process whereby the printing press and other new devices such as the telegraph and camera became generally recognized as journalistic technologies.

SIX

ELECTRIFICATION

Before 1844, the circulation of news across great distances depended on sources of transportation that were slow. In normal times, this was not a problem. But in the midst of wars and other extraordinary events, the length of time it took for news to move across vast distances was painfully obvious. After Great Britain's militia attacked and burned Washington, D.C., during the War of 1812, it took twenty-four hours for Philadelphia's residents to hear of the capitulation of the capital, three days for New York City residents, and a week for the citizens of Raleigh, North Carolina. And while the January 8, 1815, battle of New Orleans has been hailed as a great American victory, it would not have been fought if news of a recently signed peace treaty had reached military leaders. Surely, faster and more dependable news delivery was becoming a priority for any newspaper publisher with hopes of beating out the competition.

Samuel Morse's electric telegraph was heralded after its 1844 U.S. debut as a remarkable invention. A writer for the *National Intelligencer,* at Washington, D.C., called it a "wonderful result of human ingenuity," while an *Ohio Observer* newspaper report, at the town of Hudson, stated: "The advantage of this mode of communication must be obvious, both in war and peace."[171] Morse was an artist and scholar who had worked on his telegraph machine for more than a decade before he demonstrated it publicly on an electric wire erected between Washington, D.C., and Baltimore. Across the Atlantic, other inventors had been working on electric telegraph machines. In 1838, William Cooke and Charles Wheatstone developed the first electric telegraph to go into commercial service in England. But Morse's device would be the one adopted across the globe. It was based on a system in which signals were encoded within a series of dots and dashes imprinted on moving paper tape. People initially greeted the conveyance of the telegraph line's first message—"What hath God wrought?"—with awe and later with tremendous enthusiasm. Most of them were not yet familiar with electricity, let alone the concept that a small mechanical device could eliminate the impediment of distance in the sending and receiving of messages.

Morse's telegraph left an irrevocable mark on the history of journalism, although, like all radical new technologies, it did not do so by itself. The revolution triggered by the telegraph consisted of many inventions and innovations. The most significant of these involved advances in the field of science devoted to the harnessing of electricity, the foundation on which the telegraph as a technology rested. Nevertheless, through its ability to send and receive messages instantaneously, dependably, and cheaply, the telegraph rendered obsolete old news circulation practices such as those based on the pigeon and the horse-drawn carriage. Furthermore, the telegraph led to the development of a new business structure in the newspaper field: the cooperative news agency. And finally, historians contend that, in addition to fostering changes in the content and organization of the news stories it circulated, the telegraph altered people's sense of time and space as variables in the news communication process due to its remarkable quickness and ability to eliminate distance as a factor in delivering messages.

Morse's electric telegraph was preceded by at least two centuries of experimentation with "electric fluid." In 1600, English scientist William Gilbert described the electrification of many substances and coined the term *electricity* from the Greek word for amber. In 1660, Otto von Guericke invented a crude machine for producing static electricity. Later in the century, scientists created the first mechanical generators of electricity, developed the concepts of static electricity and electrical attraction and repulsion, learned that electric force was transmitted through a vacuum, and deduced that various substances were either conductors or nonconductors of electricity. In the next century, C. F. Du Fay recognized two kinds of electricity, which Benjamin Franklin and another Philadelphian named positive and negative. Franklin's famous experiments with electricity, which took place in the mid-1770s, were undoubtedly the first connection between American journalism and electricity. His interest in electricity had nothing to do with his work with newspapers, yet it is one of journalism history's most delightful ironies that a famous hero in the journalistic field was also among the earliest scientists to study electricity.

The original definition of the word *telegraph,* a verb derived from the Greek language, was "to write far" by sending a message across a great expanse of space. The electric telegraph was not the first telegraph machine used to send messages. Fifty years before Morse unveiled the electric telegraph, devices for sending messages using optical systems were invented in France and Sweden. The first of these techniques was devised by Claude Chappe, a clergyman from France, who built the earliest optical telegraph network in 1794. Chappe's system consisted of semaphore signals that depended on a signaling mechanism using a connecting section called a regulator and two pieces at the ends called indicators. With a rig of pulleys, the regulator could be situated horizontally or vertically, and the position of the indicators could be varied in increments of forty-five degrees. Chappe came up with 92 configurations and then developed a codebook with 92 pages, each with 92 lines. There were 8,464 words, letters, or phrases possible. Each was uniquely coded by two signals, the first designating the page and the second the line on the page. By 1799, two more codebooks were added and were designated by shift codes, bringing the total up to 25,392 entries. Entire messages could be transmitted in this manner across all of France in just a few minutes via telegraph stations placed about six miles apart.

The first message Chappe sent over his system in its public demonstration included the words "If you succeed, you will bask in glory." The response of the English press to his demonstration indicated the strong impression his system made on the public. The September 1794 *Gentleman's Magazine* described the new invention as

> a method to acquaint people at a great distance, and in very little time, with whatever one pleased. This method is as follows: let persons be placed in several stations, at such distances from each other, that, by the help of a telescope, a man in one station may see a signal made by the next before him; he immediately repeats this signal, which is again repeated through all the intermediate stations. This, with considerable improvements, has been adopted by the French, and denominated a Telegraphe; and, from the utility of the invention, we doubt not but it will be soon introduced in this country.[172]

Chappe's system was highly successful in France and a number of other countries for the next fifty years.

Samuel Morse is said to have conceived of the idea of a single-wire electric telegraph during conversations with fellow passengers on a steamer as he returned to the United States from his artistic studies in Europe in 1832. Five years later, he told Congress: "The greater the speed with which intelligence can be transmitted from point to point, the greater is the benefit derived to the whole community."[173] Then, in 1838, Morse obtained a patent for his invention from the U.S. government. To acquire backing from influential investors, he shared the rights to the patent and acquired a business manager. In 1843, he obtained a grant from Congress to build his experimental line between Baltimore and the nation's capital. After his famous demonstration showed his machine could telegraph messages across vast expanses of space, people called his wires lightning lines.

Morse's forty-mile telegraph line between Baltimore and Washington, D.C., was the only one in operation until early 1846, but by that time, the massive project to extend a line to every town in America was set to start. In the midst of all the ballyhoo about the telegraph's wonders, Americans became anxious for electric lines to reach their communities. As the people of Rochester, New York, waited in May 1846, a local newspaper stated: "The actual realization of the astonishing fact, that instantaneous personal conversation can be held between persons hundreds of miles apart, can only be fully attained by witnessing the wonderful fact itself."[174] By 1848, the number of miles of line had increased to two thousand; by 1850, the miles of lines totaled about twenty thousand; and a transcontinental line reached California in 1861. In 1852, the superintendent of the U.S. Census wrote: "The telegraph system [in the United States] is carried to a greater extent than in any other part of the world."[175]

In its infancy, the telegraph was used largely for the relaying of individual messages. But realizing its potential for news delivery, newspaper publishers became involved in directing its development not long after it was introduced. William Swaim, owner of a Philadelphia penny paper, the *Ledger,* assumed a position of leadership in the first commercial telegraph corporation, the Magnetic Telegraph Company. He served on its board of directors and was also its president in 1850. James Gordon Bennett, publisher of the *New York Herald,* promoted the telegraph as well. He spent thousands of dollars on dispatches, claiming that in one week alone in 1848, he spent $12,381 on seventy-nine thousand words of telegraphic content.[176]

War and political reporting were among the top priorities of those interested in securing the telegraph for the acquisition of news. With the annexation of Texas in 1845, war with Mexico became all but inevitable. At its outbreak in 1846, only 130 miles of wire extended south of the nation's capital, to Richmond, Virginia. Bennett and a group of others set up a pony express relay between Richmond and New Orleans. Their biggest scoop of the war, which was credited to the *Baltimore Sun,* was the fall of Vera Cruz. The *Sun* learned of the victory of American soldiers at Vera Cruz ahead of the War Department and telegraphed the news to notify President James K. Polk.

The story of how the telegraph became an integral part of the newspaper business was originally told by Fredrick Hudson, the *New York Herald*'s managing editor during the years in which the new technology was first adopted for use in the circulation of news. As Hudson prepared to retire from his three-decade career at the *Herald,* he decided to share the knowledge he had acquired over the long years of his tenure. Instead of following the lead of a number of his contemporaries who were publishing autobiographies, Hudson put his skills to work in the preparation of a history book. Seven years later, the results of his efforts were impressive: with his 789-page tome covering the period 1690 to 1872, Hudson followed in Isaiah Thomas's footsteps as America's second major documenter of American journalism.

Hudson's extensive tenure as the *Herald*'s managing editor afforded him an extraordinary vantage point from which to consider the impact of the telegraph and other innovations on journalism and its products. What he had observed as managing editor of one of the country's most successful newspapers was that the telegraph alone was not enough to bring about a revolution in journalism. Rather, the revolution was triggered by the combination of the telegraph and news publishers' growing need for speedier news delivery. Hudson joined the *Herald*'s staff in 1836, when the gathering of news was still largely dependent on the mail and shipping. His first position at the paper entailed collecting foreign news that arrived on steamers from across the ocean, and to be successful at it, he had to scoop his paper's competition whenever possible. As it turned out, he was so skilled at getting the news faster than his rivals that he was soon promoted to the position of managing editor.

Hudson's position as an astute observer of change in the field of journalism in the middle of the nineteenth century was enhanced in 1846 when he became a member of a group of news publishers who entered into an unprecedented agreement. In May of that year, New York City newspaper publisher Moses Yale Beach had a novel idea, born of the need to get news of America's newly declared war with Mexico. Instead of competing with rivals for news about the conflict, he asked why not cooperate in obtaining news via the telegraph? Since sharing news was a foreign concept to the owners of New York City's penny papers, whose success or failure depended on getting the news first, the suggestion must have seemed odd. But Beach figured if publishers joined to finance delivery of news using the new telegraph, the benefits would outweigh any losses. The relationship among newspapers that resulted from his gesture became the first in a series of interactions that eventually led to the formation of the Associated Press, the world's first cooperative news-gathering agency.[177]

As electric lines were erected from town to town up and down the Atlantic corridor, partnerships between newspaper publishers hungry for faster transmission of news continued to form. Frustration with the length of time it took to erect the lines led to a number of collaborations designed to hasten the delivery of news until the telegraph could take over. The Halifax Express, established in 1849, operated during the nine months it took to erect a telegraph line from St. John to Calais, Maine. Once every two weeks, a steamer bound for Boston from Liverpool, England, stopped at Halifax, Nova Scotia. During the nine-month period that the Halifax Express was in operation, its teams of pony riders picked up the mail at Halifax and covered the 144 miles to Digby Gut, where the telegraph ended, in about eight hours. Once there, the telegraph took over, and the news reached New York City thirty-six hours before the steamer made it to Boston.

Without question, the speed of the telegraph, when coupled with economic incentives, fostered cooperation between news publishers that did not exist before. But beyond this, journalism historians have not agreed on whether or how the telegraph changed the content of news stories sent out over its wires. Some have argued that the telegraph led to a less politicized news product. Early in the nineteenth century, many newspapers were tied to political parties or politicians. But according to James W. Carey, after the birth of the wire services, the telegraph "led to a fundamental change in news. It snapped the tradition of partisan journalism by forcing the wire services to generate 'objective' news, news that could be used by papers of any political stripe." In addition, Carey stated that the telegraph eliminated the letter-writing correspondent who wrote on a particular event within a richly detailed context. The telegraph, he continued, "replaced [the letter-writing correspondent] with a stringer who supplied the bare facts."[178]

Another argument concerning the effects of the telegraph on news writing (although there is little consensus among historians on this) is that it led to the creation of the inverted pyramid news story. When writing an inverted pyramid story, newspeople put the most critical facts at the top and the least important at the bottom. This style was the most commonly used news form during the first half of the twentieth century. Most of the century's journalism writing textbooks provided instruction on how to prepare this type of story.

Some historians have argued that the inverted pyramid came about as a direct result of the telegraph, while others contend its origins are connected to the news coverage of President Abraham Lincoln's assassination.[179] A third group of scholars have rejected the binary notion that the origins of the inverted pyramid are connected to only one of these factors, since, they argue, change is undoubtedly the product of multiple forces. Journalism textbook author Chip Scanlan, for example, stated that the inverted pyramid is a product of both new technology and a "changing intellectual environment that embraced realism in art, science and literature."[180]

The debates about the effects of the telegraph serve as a reminder that the causes of change in anything as complex as the news and the processes through which it is produced are difficult to pinpoint. While technologies are often connected to innovation in journalism, they rarely bring about change by themselves.

News is so strongly related to factors such as writers, readers, and external variables such as social and cultural values, intellectual traditions, and economics that it is simply impossible for it to change for only one reason.

Although new technologies rarely by themselves lead to changes in the news, they sometimes trigger effects in the industrial and occupational structures of journalism. Disputes in this regard always involve questions of who or what is in control of specific tasks or crucial resources in a particular work or industrial setting. Radio and newspaper journalists engaged in an industrial/occupational dispute over who controlled the news in a period lasting from 1922 to 1939. With the growing popularity of radio news, newspaper professionals felt threatened, and the dispute came to a head in a series of events often referred to as the press-radio war of the 1920s and 1930s.

Going back several decades, radio as a broadcasting medium emerged out of the wireless technologies of the late nineteenth century. In the 1870s, experimentation involving the transmission of wireless radio waves began, and in 1898, Guglielmo Marconi opened the world's first "wireless" factory in England. Around 1915, radio enthusiasts such as David Sarnoff began posing the idea that the new medium could be used to disseminate content to a large audience. In 1920, KDKA in Pittsburgh started the era of radio broadcasting when it began programming on a regular basis. Milestones in radio news history that followed in the next decade included the 1924 broadcast of the Democratic and Republican national conventions, the 1925 inaugural address of newly elected President Calvin Coolidge, and the 1930 launch of Lowell Thomas's radio news program.

In a 1922 article about the changes radio would bring, *New Republic* writer Bruce Bliven imagined a new world:

There will be only one orchestra left on earth, giving nightly worldwide concerts; when all universities will be combined into one super-institution, conducting courses by radio for students in Zanzibar, Kamchatka and Oskaloose; when, instead of newspapers, trained orators will dictate the news of the world day and night, and the bedtime story will be told every evening from Paris to the sleepy children of a weary world; when every person will be instantly accessible day or night to all the bores he knows, and will know them all: when the last vestiges of privacy, solitude and contemplation will have vanished into limbo.[181]

Fifteen years later, radio journalist and writer H. V. Kaltenborn stated that the "marriage of radio and the news" had brought many significant changes to the news and that its power had to be respected. He wrote:

The invention that made possible the mass audience was bound to make history. Today mere numbers and miles mean nothing. The significance of this personal, instantly audible message is not that it may be heard by millions, but that it can and does influence millions. It was this discovery, radio's personal appeal as opposed to the anonymous and unfelt impression received by the reader of cold type, that opened up channels of radio more incisive and influential than any previous media had ever known, wider and deeper than the ether waves themselves.[182]

The press-radio war started in 1922 when the Associated Press wire service issued a notice to subscribers that AP news copy was not to be used for broadcasting purposes. The notice was widely ignored, however, since many of early radio stations were owned by large papers. In addition, other wire services said they would continue to provide copy to all their subscribers. The war heated up considerably in 1933 when a document known as the Biltmore Agreement was publicized. The newspaper industry sought to limit radio news broadcasters in a number of significant ways. This document confined the radio networks to only two five-minute newscasts per day. The newscasts had to be broadcast in the mornings, but only after 9:30 A.M., and in the evenings, but later than 9:00 P.M. There could be copy only from the established wire services, and no breaking or up-to-the-minute news could be broadcast. Finally, the agreement stipulated that radio news could not have any advertising support and that listeners were to be encouraged to consult their newspapers for the latest news.[183]

The impetus of the Biltmore Agreement was clear: the publishers recognized that radio could—and probably would—take revenue away from newspapers. The agreement allowed the networks access to some wire service content, but it restricted the broadcast content to a format that would (1) be long enough only to whet the information appetites of the news-consuming public, (2) not interfere in the prime newspaper-selling periods of morning and evening, and (3) not compete with newsrooms for advertising dollars.

In the years following the agreement, broadcasters redefined how they presented news. The document said nothing about commentary, and one of the first things that ensued was an announcement that henceforth, network radio on-air newspeople were commentators rather than broadcast reporters. Consequently, they could be sponsored. After that, it didn't take long for the agreement to crumble. Independent radio stations led the way, and much critical commentary was heard on the network airwaves. While the press war would officially end in 1939, its effects on radio news broadcasting were significant.

Radio journalism experienced the heights of its golden era during World War II. Correspondents were broadcasting from the rooftops of London as sirens announced the arrival of Nazi fighter planes, and their reports poured in from other parts of Europe. Across the Atlantic, Americans couldn't stop listening as broadcasters such as Edward R. Murrow, Charles Collingwood, Eric Sevareid, and William Shirer made them feel like they were there as well. But it would not be long before radio faced a threat that would eventually rob it of its on-air personalities and revenue stream—television.

Experimentation with television started in the 1920s, and the first demonstration of live television was aired on January 16, 1926, in London. By 1939, television was ready to be unveiled at the New York World's Fair. During the war, television was essentially put on hold, but afterward, it was set to be all the rage in America. The trade magazine *Variety* likened the new medium to a moviehouse monster, calling television the Frankenstein of radio. In the 1940s and 1950s, television attracted many of the radio's shows and personalities. Well-known radio newspeople, including Murrow, Fred Friendly, and Douglas Edwards, went over to television, and their former radio audiences followed them. To stay alive, radio had to reinvent itself. It continued to broadcast the news but adopted a sound-bite approach that emphasized immediate breaking news.

The growth of television in the 1950s was impressive. In 1952, the percentage of American homes with a television was just over 34; by the end of the decade, the number had risen to 86 percent. During this period, television became the dominant force in the American political process. Coast-to-coast broadcasting was made possible with the development of coaxial cable, and by 1951, a relay system had been established across the continent. By the

1960s, most Americans got their news from television, as radio and newspapers continued to suffer declines in revenues. The CBS, NBC, and ABC networks were in positions of great power in the broadcast news business.

Satellite and cable technologies presented a new threat in the world of broadcasting with the launch of Ted Turner's Cable News Network (CNN) in 1980. Turner was the creator of "superstation" WTBS in Atlanta. He had earlier used a satellite to offer cable stations sports and reruns of movies. Turner began the satellite service in 1976, a year after Home Box Office's successful satellite and cable experiments. In a direct challenge to the big three networks, CNN's twenty-four-hour service included hourly news summaries, heavy treatment of sports and business, news specials, and lengthy interviews on various subjects throughout the day. Initially, viewers were not impressed, but within a decade, the network had gained considerable recognition for its reporting and overall programming.

As cable has grown, new networks offering round-the-clock news have put additional strain on the three networks. Today, the Fox News network and MSNBC are also having an impact, as are a variety of news shows on Music Television (MTV) and Comedy Central targeted at specific demographics and lifestyles. All these developments are following a pattern that has been evident in broadcasting since the 1920s and 1930s. As broadcasting, satellite, and cable technologies have emerged over in the intervening years, they have threatened their immediate predecessors. Thus, the story of electrification in journalism has been one of technological challenges and periods of adjustment during which older news systems have either found find ways to reinvent themselves or disappeared.

◈

SEVEN

VISUALIZING THE NEWS

Imagine not being able to turn on the news to see the latest on-the-scene images of Hurricane Katrina or of voting for a presidential candidate whose face you had never seen. Two hundred years ago, few would have thought much about being deprived of such pictures because the news was acquired through reading and by word of mouth. The camera had not yet been invented, and the only visuals printed in newspapers were a few woodcuts and lithographs. But in 1839, Louis Jacques-Mandé's invention of the daguerreotype, the world's first photographic image, was formally announced in Paris. It would be more than forty years before the halftone process was invented, making it possible to reproduce photographs in printed newspapers and magazines. But this announcement signified a new era in which the public no longer had to depend on artists' renderings of events and people to "see" the news that took place away from home. As one historian put it: "The introduction of newspaper photography was a phenomenon of immense importance, one that changed the outlook of the masses. . . . Photography opened a window, as it were. The faces of public personalities became familiar and things that happened all over the globe were his to share. As the reader's outlook expanded, the world began to shrink."[184]

Photography's "window on the world" was eventually extended even further with the introductions of subsequent visual technologies, including the moving picture, television, satellite, and the World Wide Web, along with a host of associated devices. And electricity, the computer, and digitization have also played a part in the transformation of journalism into a more visual product. But a complete history of this "visual revolution" requires studying image technologies that existed long before the camera, as well as the effects of social, cultural, and economic conditions that have influenced the history of visual journalism.

The woodcut was the first in a long line of technologies that eventually led to the blossoming of photojournalism in the twentieth century. First used by people in East Asian cultures to create and reproduce symbols, designs, and pictures, the Chinese woodblock was the forerunner of those eventually used in newspapers. A technique developed for printing text or images sometime between the mid-sixth century and the late ninth century, woodblock printing involved three ingredients—the printing block, which carried the design; ink, which was widely used in early China; and paper, which was first developed in China around the third or second century B.C.[185]

Artisans create woodcuts by removing the wood around the lines or shapes that together form the desired printed image. Images in this relief process are produced by inking the raised surfaces and pressing them against paper or some other material, either manually or by running them through a press. As early as the eighth century, the Chinese used the technique of stamping from woodblocks to print textiles; later, they used woodblocks for illustrating books. Indeed, the Chinese used woodblock printing to create the world's earliest dated printed book, the Diamond Sutra, in A.D. 868. The ancient Egyptians and Babylonians used woodcuts to press intaglio designs on bricks, and the Romans used them for stamping letters and symbols.

Woodcuts were used in Europe at the beginning of the fifteenth century, when enterprising craftspeople began to create religious pictures for distribution to pilgrims; they also used them on playing cards and simple prints and for the block books that preceded the works produced on Gutenberg's printing press. One of the first dated European woodcuts is an image of St. Christopher from 1423. Hundreds of years passed between the first use of woodcuts by printers and their regular use by publishers of the news. But before the appearance of the earliest newspapers in the fifteenth and sixteenth centuries, printers sometimes included woodcuts in the broadsides that came off their presses. Similar to pamphlets, broadsides contained news of important or otherwise interesting events. In 1595, for example, a broadside that told the story of a famous siege at Sulina, Romania, was published with a woodcut.

Colonial America's printers also used woodcuts in their broadsides. During the American Revolution, broadsides were prominently employed in reporting and commentary by those both for and against a political break with Great Britain. In the early stages of the Revolution, for example, in reaction to the Stamp Act of 1765, broadsides decorated with images of the public hangings of the effigy of the stamp man were published by individuals across the colonies who wanted to protest England's imposition of the tax.

After the Revolution, printers continued to use woodcuts in not only in their broadsides but also in a host of other printed materials disseminating newsworthy information and ideas about controversial events and people. In 1815, for instance, a booklet relating the story of the kidnapping of an American woman by Native Americans was published in Providence, Rhode Island. The image showed three native men, one with a bow and arrow, facing three American men, two armed with rifles.[186]

Newspaper publisher John Campbell marked one momentous occasion with another on January 19, 1707, when he published the first woodcut illustration included in an American newspaper in one of the columns of his *Boston News-Letter.*[187] The event Campbell wished to commemorate was the political marriage of his native Scotland with England. The woodcut printed in the *News-Letter* was a rendering of the new flag designed to symbolize the merging of the two countries. Although Scotland kept its independence with respect to its legal and religious systems, subsumed in the union were its parliament, coinage, taxation, sovereignty, and trade. The flag, thereafter referred to as the Union Jack, combined the red cross of St. George with the blue cross of St. Andrew.

It is easy to imagine that the appearance of the flag in the *News-Letter* provoked discussion among those who frequented Boston's coffeehouses and taverns. The new political arrangement was a subject of great controversy in Scotland, where public opinion was weighted heavily against it. Considered by some to be one of history's earliest journalists because of the stories he wrote about important events, Daniel Defoe's initial accounts of the reaction of the Scots told of violent demonstrations against the act. "A Scots rabble is the worst of its kind, for every Scot in favour there is 99 against," he reported.[188]

Since the demands of periodic publishing made it impossible for printers to include more than a few woodcut images in their early prints, those that were used are especially notable. Benjamin Franklin's insertion of a set of images in an issue of the *Pennsylva-*

nia Gazette in 1745 was an early and rare example of a news-related graphic accompanied by a didactic editorial comment. The illustrations, which included an image of a fortress at Louisbourg and a map, accompanied a written account about the broadening of Britain's dispute with Spain into the War of Austrian Succession. To explain, Franklin wrote: "As the CAPE-BRETON expedition is at present the Subject of most conversations, we hope the following Draught (rough as it is, for want of good Engravers here) will be acceptable to our Readers; as it may serve to give them an Idea of the Strength and Situation of the Town now besieged by our Forces, and render the News we receive from thence more intelligible."[189]

More common in colonial newspapers were small, mainly decorative woodcuts inserted without commentary in multiple issues. In 1719, for example, the publisher of the *Boston Gazette* added an illustration of a ship to the left of the front page's title, along with one of a trumpet riding a running horse to its right.[190] Although not related to the day's news, images of ships and horses conveyed the idea that the paper's purpose was to transport news. Around the same time, newspaper publishers began to use small, topically appropriate woodcuts in conjunction with advertisements. Images of ships, scythes and sickles, books, and clock faces were among the most common, as were illustrations of running African Americans alongside announcements of runaway slaves.

Franklin's earliest newspaper illustrations were connected to nonpolitical events, but they assumed a more partisan complexion as the political environment became more charged. What is generally considered to be America's earliest printed cartoon was published in a 1747 pamphlet titled *Plain Truth*. Anonymously written and printed by Benjamin Franklin, the pamphlet's purpose was to persuade Pennsylvanians to arm themselves against the threat of violence posed by the French. With the caption "The Waggoner and Hercules," the cartoon portrayed a team bogged in mire, with the driver praying to Zeus for help; Zeus, sitting on his cloud, did nothing. Its obvious moral was that God helps those who help themselves.

The impending crisis was precipitated by rumors circulating in Philadelphia during the final stages of King George's War when French privateers began appearing off the coast of British America. In July 1747, a French vessel went so far as to enter Delaware Bay, where it damaged some shipping and even sent a raiding party ashore near Newcastle. The French were said to have knowledge of the navigation of the river and of the fact that six privateers would be sent to attack the defenseless city of Philadelphia the next spring. When the assembly refused to take the situation seriously, a group of merchants raised a sum for fitting out a privateer.[191] At that moment, Franklin came forward with an elaborate plan for defense. "I determined," he later wrote in his autobiography, "to try what might be done by a voluntary Association of the People."[192]

In 1754, his most famous cartoon, "Join or Die," became the first to appear in a newspaper.[193] The image portrayed a snake in eight pieces, each labeled with the initial of one of the colonies along the eastern shore of America. Its caption was designed to prod the colonists into defending the British against the French and their Native American allies. By that time, engraving on metal rather than wood was more commonly used for cartoons and more elaborate caricatures.

These early cartoons were the direct outgrowth of crises that affected all colonists, but by the mid-1760s, the objective character of the cartoons disappeared when their creators began using them as agents for partisan campaigning and protests against British authority. In the Pennsylvania election of 1764, candidates representing all factions used cartoons. One of the cleverest of the cartoon artists was David Dove, a Quaker schoolmaster who deployed his talents in the service of the Quaker party.

After the Stamp Act controversy broke out in 1765, several of Paul Revere's cartoons were published in Boston newspapers, including his famous "Tree of Liberty." As an engraver, Revere incised designs into metal plates by applying pressure with a pointed tool called a graver or burin. The earliest known line engravings were issued in the fifteenth century. Revere is best known as a silversmith, but his talents as a highly skilled copper engraver were put to use in the propaganda war against the British. The caption accompanying his cartoon image referred to the honoring of the tree "upon which the Effigies of a Stamp Master was lately hung."[194]

Four copperplate images made by Revere and published by Franklin in 1764 and 1765 are notable examples of how engraving was used to send messages about the political events of the day. All four included a group of armed volunteers amassed in front of the Old Philadelphia Courthouse to fight the notorious Paxton Boys, a group of frontiersmen who had massacred some peaceful Conestoga Indians living near white settlements in Lancaster. The Paxton Boys were enraged that the government seemed to be doing little to help those who lived near the violence.

Shortly before the Revolution, Revere engraved a cartoon for Franklin titled "The Colonies Reduced," showing England's symbol fallen from her place of prominence on the globe. Britannia was portrayed as a woman leaning against a globe and surrounded by her severed limbs, labeled with the names of various colonies. Franklin hoped his representation of Britain's lowered state would sway its leaders toward a more lenient colonial policy.

As the nineteenth century progressed, political cartoons grew in number and popularity. One of America's first major cartoon artists was William Charles (1776–1820), a Scottish immigrant who settled in Philadelphia in 1806 after he was prosecuted for publishing an unflattering caricature of a local official.[195] Like Paul Revere, Charles created metal engravings rather than woodcuts. As a result, he was able to make more complex drawings than were possible with woodcuts at the time. Charles's drawings were so complex and often so politically vicious that they helped popularize the cartoon as a journalistic element. One of his most famous— "The Tory Editor and His Apes Giving Their Pitiful Advice to American Sailors"—was published in 1808, the product of his frustration with the conditions that led up to the War of 1812.

Charles's inclusion of dialogue between his cartoons' characters must have inspired the imaginations of those who saw them. In 1814, his "Johnny Bull and the Alexandrians" portrayed England as a bull dressed up and on its hind legs, saying: "I must have all your Flour—All your Tobacco—All your Provisions—All your ships—All your Merchandize—Every thing except your Porter and Perry keep them out of my sight, I've had enough of them alright." In response, a "Yankey" said: "Pray Mr. Bull don't be too hard with us—you know we were always friendly, even in time of your Embargo!"

Cartoonists and other illustrators also produced images using a technique called wood engraving, a process akin to both the woodcut and the metal-engraving process that was developed in England by Thomas Bewick (1753–1828). Trained as a metal engraver, Bewick applied the tools of metal engraving to the hard end grain of boxwood blocks. The drawing and carving process was labor intensive and expensive, but the image produced could then be printed cheaply and quickly by letterpress at the same time as text.

Wood engraving was a practical means of reproducing images in periodicals because, unlike steel- and copperplate engraving, it produced images that did not have to be printed separately on single sheets. Instead, images made with wood engravings could be integrated with text on both sides of sheets. This process fostered a further development of pictorial reporting, wherein printers incorporated engravings with particular stories on the same page.

Another phase in the history of American editorial cartoons was inspired by the development of lithography, a faster process than the one used to make woodcuts and engravings. Cartoon lithography flourished in America after it first appeared in 1829. The primary producers of lithographs were the firms of Henry R. Robinson and Currier and Ives. As the Civil War approached, Currier and Ives marketed cartoons related to both sides of the day's controversial issues.

Among the most notable cartoonists from this period were Thomas Nast (1840–1902), Joseph Keppler (1838–1894), and Walter McDougall (1884–1952), who became famous when their politically scathing cartoons appeared in the period's illustrated dailies and weeklies. Historians regard one of McDougall's cartoons as among the most effective in U.S. history. Intended to comment on the 1884 candidacy of James G. Blaine for president, "Belshazzar's Feast" portrayed the candidate feasting on "lobby pudding" and "monopoly soup" at an extravagant dinner at Delmonico's restaurant in New York City.

From Benjamin Franklin's woodcuts to the cartoons of Nast, Keppler, and McDougall, those who published images in the newspapers used them to express opinion rather than accompany news stories. Yet they helped pave the way to the illustrated newspapers of the mid-nineteenth century. Such periodicals differed from the day's regular newspapers in that their primary emphasis was on graphic rather than literary representations of the news. One of America's first illustrated weeklies was the *New York Mirror,* which was started in 1823. But not until the 1850s were conditions right for the illustrated periodicals to become widely popular. In the decade before the Civil War, the famous *Harper's Weekly* and *Frank Leslie's Illustrated Newspaper,* among others, were launched.

Frank Leslie started one of the most popular pictorial periodicals in America in 1855. Born Henry Carter in England, he had established himself as a highly skilled engraver at the *Illustrated London News.* After arriving in the United States in 1848, he built up numerous publishing enterprises, some of which had little success. The one venture that far exceeded all his other projects was a pictorial weekly that he named after himself: *Frank Leslie's Illustrated Newspaper.* This paper was the first successful American journalistic venture to favor pictures over written text. On Leslie's death in 1880, his wife and business partner, Miriam Leslie, changed her name to Frank Leslie and kept the paper until 1902. It was continued under the same name by its new owner until 1922, when it was subsumed in a merger with a periodical called *Judge.*

Leslie employed more than one hundred artists, engravers, and printers in his New York City publishing headquarters. Out of concern that his employees labor in the kind of atmosphere that would be conducive to excellent work, he wrote: "An illustrated newspaper, if it fulfills its mission, must have its employees under constant excitement. There can be no indolence or ease about such an establishment. Every day brings its allotted and Herculean task, and night affords no respite."[196]

The process of creating illustrated news stories was long and complex. Each story began with the dispatching of an artist-reporter who, as he observed the news, drew visual impressions of events with a few rapid strokes, which were accompanied by notes

jotted down on the sketch itself. A completed drawing was transmitted back to the office in New York by the quickest means
available. After receiving editorial approval, the image was transformed through a series of steps into a finished engraving. This
process started when an artist copied and improved on the reporter's original drawing in reverse, transferring it onto one or
more woodblocks (most often made of hard Turkish boxwood).
The work was continued by different artists, whose improvements
on the original were called finishings. The image was then sent to
an engraver, who carefully removed the wood around the lines
that had been drawn. When inked, this relief block produced what
was known as a black-line facsimile engraving. The last stage in the
process involved a master engraver, who was responsible for making further decisions about the stylistic direction the whole image
should take. Once the piece was finished, the master engraver gave
the block to one of his assistants, who would complete the task
under his direction.

In line with one of his mottos, "Never shoot over the reader's
head," Leslie drove his staff to produce stories that catered to the
tastes of as many members of the public as possible. Knowing
the public in the East was curious about the westward migration,
the paper from time to time included stories about the experiences
and circumstances of those who headed west to establish new
communities. Reports of violent conflict in the West involving
Native Americans, western settlers, and the military were included
periodically. The growing problem of urban crime along with stories on the industrial strikes and riots that hit the country during
the last half of the nineteenth century were featured prominently
in the paper. The Civil War, however, was the event that made
all the difference in the fortunes of the paper. During the conflict,
Leslie sent cadres of artist-reporters across the front to depict all of

the principal engagements. In doing so, his press brought visual news to audiences hungry to learn what was happening on the battlefields, in military camps, and at military headquarters. Leslie's Civil War readers appreciated the quickness with which his staff reproduced images depicting war-front scenes. Using his team of expert engravers, Leslie was able to perfect his system so that he sometimes could publish pictures of events only a week old.

Leslie believed illustrations created through the work of artists who went out into the field to sketch what they saw were superior to ones based on photographs. Although photography was in its infancy and some illustrators used photos as a basis for their images, Leslie preferred the drawings of his artists. He argued against the use of photographs in the creation of illustrations in the April 2, 1859, edition of his paper, where he wrote: "We do not depend upon the accidental transmission of photographs, with their corpse-like literalness, but upon our own special artists."

Although the era of the illustrated newspapers overlapped with that of the photograph in 1839, forty years passed before it was possible to print photos as news. Newspapers and magazines did not reproduce photographic images until 1880, when the invention of the halftone process made this possible. Photography started with the daguerreotype, which quickly became popular for the taking of portraits. But not until inventors were able to overcome photography's technical limitations was it possible to use it for other purposes. The earliest photographic equipment was large and cumbersome, and as a result, most photos were taken in studios rather than on the scene of the events being covered. Also complicating the photographic process was the length of time it took a camera's lens to capture the image taken by the photographer. This delay meant it was impossible to capture live action with the earliest cameras. Despite these problems, however, Leslie and the period's other publishers of illustrated newspapers contributed to the development of photojournalism by creating the expectation among the public that news could be conveyed not simply through written words but also through images.

Historians have identified the work of Mathew B. Brady, Alexander Gardner, and Timothy O'Sullivan as the first photography that can be considered journalistic rather than primarily for portraiture. During the Civil War, Brady and his entourage of assistants and equipment, for example, became a familiar sight at Civil War battlegrounds and military camps, where they took pictures of living and dead soldiers and horses, destroyed buildings, and devastated landscapes. Brady's black wagon became so associated with death that some claim Union soldiers dreaded seeing it come into their camps.[197]

The first newspaper photograph printed using the new halftone screen process was titled "Shantytown" and appeared in the *New York Daily Graphic* on March 4, 1880. The photo, which captured the image of one of the many shanty homes that were cropping up in some of the city's poorest neighborhoods, was part of a story about how photographs were currently being used and reproduced in the publishing business. Not for several decades, however, would newspapers routinely include photographs reproduced with halftones instead of the drawings made using photographs or by artist-reporters on the spot. In 1919, with the launching of New York's *Illustrated Daily News,* American newspapers began to feature photographs routinely. Fueling this trend were lighter, handheld cameras and faster lenses.

Early in the twentieth century, when the Progressive movement fostered an environment friendlier to the idea of photography as a social force, photojournalism began to coalesce into a news field with wide public impact. Two photographers often given credit for the development of the field of photojournalism in that period are Lewis Hine and Jacob Riis. A native of Wisconsin, Hine went to New York City in 1901, where he found an urban landscape teeming with immigrants, many of whom arrived in the city with nothing but what they could carry. He became a photographer for the National Child Labor Committee in 1908 and took many realistic photos of children who were exploited in the factories and other workplaces. Jacob Riis, a *New York Herald* police reporter, also employed realistic, hard-hitting photographs to illustrate articles he wrote calling for social reform. He is famous for his book of photographs titled *How the Other Half Lives: Studies among the Tenements of New York* (1890). By early in the twentieth century, the formation of photo agencies and technological developments including the halftone and the handheld camera had contributed to the evolution of the photojournalism profession. Despite the coalescence of a professional association, many members of the public to this day have little respect for photojournalists, who, they complain, invade people's privacy.

By early in the twentieth century, photojournalism had become a major element of newspaper and magazine reporting. Other factors affecting the development of this field included the public's interest in photographs, the photojournalistic coverage of certain pivotal events, and the emergence of photo agencies designed to forward the interests of those involved in the new field of photojournalism. And like still photography, motion pictures eventually came to be used for the dissemination of news. Although the use of film for newsreels, as they became known, was short-lived compared to still-photographic technologies, the newsreels were a significant source of news for many Americans from 1911 to the 1960s. The earliest films that could be called newsreels were actualités, that is, true-life events filmed outdoors by the first cameras.

Beginning in 1895, short films depicting sports and political events were shown in America's fledgling community of motion picture theaters. A milestone in the history of the newsreel took place in 1911, when the Pathé Company began to release new films on a weekly basis. The public had developed a taste for newsreels by World War I. In the sound era after 1926, there were five big newsreel companies: Fox Movietone, Paramount, Universal, Warner-Pathé (owned by RKO after 1931), and Hearst Metrotone. In addition, each month, *March of Time,* a newsreel that resembled a newsmagazine, was shown in theaters across America. The famous newsreel story of the Hindenberg explosion, on May 6, 1937, became infamous as one of this era's most notable journalistic coups.

After the newsreel reached its prime in the 1930s and the war years of the 1940s, it declined in popularity as television brought visual news into homes. The *March of Time* documentary was transferred to television in 1951, and television's first regular news broadcast, *CBS TV News,* began in 1948. And just as television news eclipsed the newsreel, it contributed to a decline in the popularity of radio news. Television news, however, was not an entirely new product. In fact, its creators took from both of their visual news predecessors in their efforts to win audiences. According to Kristine Brunovska Karnick: "NBC experimented with several different formats for the presentation of television news. One approach had its roots in the broadcasting of news on radio, and another was rooted in the theatrical newsreel."[198]

It would take much more than this, however, for television news to thrive. Early television news, for example, with its dependence on news reading, was considered by many to be visually dull. And this was but one of the complex problems that TV news producers had to address.

A strategy used at times by the owners of television to increase their success was to invest in new technologies with the potential to deliver more viewers. The development of videotape was an especially appealing tool for television news producers, and CBS News began to use it in 1945 on its new Douglas Edwards show. In 1962, AT&T launched the first communication satellite, and in 1965, one was used for commercial purposes for the first time. In 1969, *Apollo 11* transmitted live TV pictures from the surface of the moon. Perhaps inspired by this event, Ted Turner's CNN would depend heavily on satellites.

The development of videotape technologies in the 1960s affected television news. The Ampex Corporation introduced videotape at a 1956 CBS-TV affiliates' session. By 1968, a few television news producers had outfitted their reporters with portable camera equipment.[199] In 2000, TV cameraman Frank Beacham described how he reacted the first time he saw a portable camera: "It was a sight that astonished me. A young Japanese reporter carried a portable black and white television camera and recorder on his shoulder. This miniature, body-worn TV studio was called a 'Portapak.'" As one writer on this era of TV news put it: "Back in 1968, all TV news was shot on 16mm film; many TV studio cameras in that era were seemingly as large as Volkswagen Beetles. Cables extending from these cameras were thicker than many human arms and, quite literally, weighed tons!"[200]

Television's adoption of wireless technologies since the mid-1990s has helped reporters broadcast from places they could not get to with cameras before. Although the national conventions of the political parties do not attract as many viewers as they used to, competition has encouraged networks to upgrade their technologies whenever possible. In 2000, CBS News Director Eric Shapiro discussed a crew's placement at the Democratic National Convention of a pencil-size camera in the scenery behind the speaker's podium. Shapiro said: "It gave a panoramic view of the floor. The resolution is not as good but it is something a little special, it gives a little added value. All the networks try and do things like this."[201]

The emergence of videotape technologies for news gathering has opened up new opportunities for private citizens to become involved in journalism. In fact, some of the biggest news stories of the late twentieth century developed in reaction to the use of such technologies by an ordinary citizen with an eye for a story. Reporter and independent media maker Lawrence Richette commented on this at a 1999 Philadelphia City Council hearing held to get citizen input on the enforcement of the city's cable television public access ordinance. He said: "The most important videotape shot in the past decade in America was not made by commercial television. It was the videotape on a camcorder of Rodney King being beaten by the Los Angeles Police Department. That videotape of Rodney King [was] shot, as I said, by a private citizen, who then had to go shop it around to the local news departments of Los Angeles. And it almost did not make it onto local Los Angeles TV."[202]

The world's first communication satellites were launched into orbit in 1962, and later that year, U.S. Vice President Lyndon Johnson took the first telephone call from space. In 1963, Tokyo's Olympic Games were broadcast via satellite, and in 1965, a satellite was used for commercial purposes for the first time. *Early Bird,* as it was known, handled communications for those who produced telephone, television, telegraph, and facsimile transmissions. In 1969, *Apollo 11* transmitted pictures from the surface of the moon. Today, satellites are a crucial component of a news delivery system that offers real-time news around the clock every day of the year.

Broadcast technology did not deliver signals to people outside its range, but the development and eventual spread of cable systems throughout the United States allowed a much bigger audience to receive television. America's first cable television transmissions were the result of "simple amateur ingenuity."[203] People who lived in remote rural areas and the mountains could not receive broadcast signals, and in 1948, the operators of an appliance store in Mahanoy City, Pennsylvania, decided to do something about it. After adding television to their store's inventory, John and Mary Walson began hearing from customers who were having problems receiving clear signals from three nearby Philadelphia network stations. In response, John Walson erected an antenna on a utility pole atop a nearby mountain and connected it to his appliance store using a cable and modified signal boosters. After demonstrating the clear signals that cable delivered, Walson connected the televisions of several of his customers who lived along the cable's path to the antenna.

During the 1950s and 1960s, other remote communities were provided with cable through the efforts of local entrepreneurs and citizen groups. By 1960, there were 640 systems with 650,000 subscribers; a decade later, the number had grown to 2,490 systems with 4.5 million subscribers.[204]

Programming on early cable was retransmitted broadcast fare, but eventually, services unique to cable developed. As cable-programming entrepreneurs began to experiment with the concept of narrowcasting, they established channels that targeted particular demographic groups, including children, teenagers, women, and racial and ethnic groups. In addition, channels that targeted viewers interested in special topics were developed, and some of them became lucrative.

The concept of an all-news channel gained the attention of cable entrepreneur Ted Turner, and in 1980, he launched CNN, a twenty-four-hour-a-day, seven-days-a-week phenomenon with an emphasis on national and international news. Eventually, Turner's success would be shared by others interested in providing national and international news at all hours of the day. In 1996, NBC and Microsoft joined hands in the establishment of MSNBC, and also in that year, Fox News Channel appeared on the air for the first time.

In the mid-1980s, local and regional news providers began to think about establishing their own all-news channels. Before 1986, local television news in America was almost exclusively the preserve of local broadcast stations, primarily the affiliates of what were then known as the "big three" networks, ABC, CBS, and NBC. But in December of that year, Cablevision Systems Corporation unveiled News 12 Long Island, the first twenty-four-hour local/regional cable news channel in the country. Today, nearly forty cable systems across America offer local and regional news channels, including systems in a majority of the top twenty television markets.

In the mid-1990s, new digital photographic equipment precipitated a technology-driven debate over the question of whether photojournalists should go digital. Some news photographers answered the question with a resounding No. But a growing number of photojournalists were saying just the opposite. Reporting that their new digital cameras offered tremendous advantages over their old equipment, they said they would never go back. After nostalgically professing his love for "the sheer beauty of a fine silver print from film exposed in a conventional camera," the publisher of a Web site started in 1997 titled the Digital Journalist asked the critics of new cameras to think twice before dismissing them out of hand. He wrote: "It probably was the same when the printing press came around. A large group of people probably said the Gutenberg Bible just wasn't the same as the beautiful, hand-lettered and illuminated bibles that the monks over in Italy were turning out. That's correct. But for the people who were able to read the stories in the Bible for the first time, it probably didn't seem too important. And for the story tellers themselves, the more, the merrier."[205]

Behind the development of history's earliest digital imaging technology were the space exploration and government surveillance programs of the 1950s and 1960s. The history of the digital camera can also be traced to the development of videotape recording. In the 1970s, some still photographers began to explore the possibility of using video and electronic imaging in photojournalism. One of the first to publish work in digital form was *National Geographic* photographer Emory Kristof, who used an electronic camera in a 1979 story that took him to the bottom of the ocean in a miniature submarine.[206]

Forty years later, pioneers in the desktop publishing boom began to apply such digital surveillance technologies to the photographic images published in newspapers and magazines. The very first of the new digital cameras, which began to appear in the early 1990s, did not offer many advantages over other cameras, and according to one writer, they were only the "playthings of creative types working in design studios."[207] In the mid-1990s, however, Kodak began releasing a series of cameras with greater potential for professional photographers. One of their earliest models, the DSC 460, generated a lot of discussion among camera aficionados. The camera, which sold for $12,000, was a standard single-lens reflex model with a clip-on device that enabled the capturing of digital images with a resolution of 6.2 megapixels. To collect information on people's responses to its new line of cameras, Kodak started an online forum that still operates today. Since March 1, 1995, the forum has generated tens of thousands of hits within more than five thousand discussion threads.[208]

That our memories of history's most powerful news-related images tend to be long is testament to the fact that photographs and other visual records of events can hold great power. Ask any American who lived during the Vietnam War era, for example, to think of a memorable photograph, and images come readily to mind. In response, some scholars and critics have long been concerned about the social, psychological, and cultural powers of visual news. Others have been concerned about the power that is conferred on those who practice visual journalism. Susan Sontag, the author of a famous book titled *On Photography,* wrote: "To take a photograph is to participate in another person's mortality, vulnerability, mutability. Precisely by slicing out this moment and freezing it, all photographs testify to time's relentless melt."[209] Still others are worried about the potential ethical problems associated with visual news. In the era of digital photographic technologies, the manipulation of news images is commonplace but problematic.

Just how visual technologies have impacted journalism across history is difficult to measure. But as visual technologies have been adopted by journalists, it seems inevitable that the print and broadcast news stories they become part of will be quantitatively and qualitatively altered as a result. Also of interest is the role of human agency in the social construction of visual news. As in the case of newspapers, it is reasonable to suggest that the visual news product of any particular publisher is, in some measure, a social construction of the public that consumes it.

EIGHT

FROM DESKTOP TO DIGITAL

As the age of new media emerged in the 1980s, America appeared to have lost the optimism that had been a hallmark of its culture for generations. Many citizens felt deep concern about the health of the nation and its future. Interest in politics was waning. Literacy was dropping. Race was still a troublesome issue. And the labor movement was losing its power. Just as everything seemed to be falling away, new technologies were starting to make an appearance, and they seemed to be offering some hope:

> At last, through the digital computer and through data services, information technology has united all media and forms of information. In the future, all will be served by the same technology, and all will be integrated in our life, work and recreation.[210]

> The idea is that the changes through which we are now going are every bit as tremendous as those which transformed the world of local communities based on subsistence agriculture into the world of sprawling cities, machines, mills, and factories.[211]

> The old world of the industrial revolution that we inherited
> from the past is clearly in upheaval. This chaotic period is cer-
> tainly creating serious difficulties. But this period of chaos is a
> fertile one, for the chaos is caused by the coming of a tremen-
> dous new age.[212]

But could computers resolve the pressing problems of the day?
James W. Carey had already asked that question in 1973 in an
essay titled "The History of the Future." He wrote: "Despite the
manifest failure of technology to resolve pressing social issues over
the last century, contemporary intellectuals continue to see revolutionary potential in the latest technological gadgets that are pictured as a force outside history and politics."[213] Like the experts
who have found so much hope in the computer, many in the field
of journalism have looked to the adoption of computer and Internet technologies in hopes of banishing the profession's and the
industry's doldrums. Newsrooms replaced their old-fashioned
typewriters and typesetting machines and were using video display terminals and word-processing systems. Almost all aspects of
the newsroom's operation, including production, layout, composition, circulation, and the newspaper archive, were computerized. But more help was needed. In the 1980s and 1990s, professional journalism was suffering from a lack of credibility stemming
from a variety of sources, among them Vietnam, Pulitzer Prize
embarrassments, and the backlash against liberalism. These concerns were bothering journalists.

Looking for a way to use computers for more than just word
processing, journalists began to explore the potential of a news-
gathering and analysis process called computer-assisted reporting.
The concept is a broad one and includes any use of computers in
the collection and interpretation of news. The earliest computer-

assisted stories entailed mining data compiled from reports generated from computer databases. The first story that used computers was published during the 1952 presidential election. When the election was predicted to be a close race, a group of CBS reporters decided to use a Remington Rand UNIVAC computer for help in predicting its outcome based on early returns. When the computer indicated that Dwight Eisenhower was winning by a landslide, the network was reluctant to broadcast what the reporters had learned. When it finally did, it was ridiculed for not reporting earlier what the computer had revealed.

Twenty years later, a growing number of reporters were taking advantage of computerized databases in their stories. In a major 1973 book on the use of computers in journalism, University of North Carolina professor Philip Meyer stated that computers were enabling journalists to become more scientific. According to Meyer, journalists who skillfully used computers were practicing "precision journalism."[214]

Eventually, the development of the Internet and desktop computers with considerable processing capabilities aided reporters with an interest in computer-assisted reporting. In 1989, the National Institute for Computer-Assisted Reporting was formed. Its objective was to train journalists "in the practical skills of finding, prying loose, and analyzing electronic information."[215]

Today, computer-assisted reporting is a complex and sophisticated area within the field of journalism. College programs and institutes designed to further education and research in this area have been started all over the world. Computer-assisted news stories are being published on a diverse array of topics, such as finance, health care, politics, the environment, and government. The technique is especially helpful in projects that require analysis of a large volume of records or data.

Desktop publishing is another application of computers in journalism that emerged in the mid-1980s. Using computer software, desktop publishers format and combined text, numerical data, photographs, charts, and other visual graphic elements to produce publication-ready material. Depending on the nature of a particular project, they may write and edit text, create graphics to accompany text, convert photographs and drawings into digital images and then manipulate those images, design page layouts, create proposals, develop presentations and advertising campaigns, typeset and do color separations, and translate electronic information onto film or other traditional forms.

Before desktop computers, it cost hundreds of thousands of dollars to establish a printing press. According to cyberspace columnist Paul Bissex: "What made this little 'revolution' so exciting to some was not that a better technology had come along (after all, when phototypesetting replaced 'hot metal' composition it hardly inspired a popular movement), but that it had come along in such a seemingly democratic form. Coupled with the cheap reproduction offered by the photocopier, DTP looked like a big break for the 'little guy.'"[216]

The initial high cost of the equipment dropped sharply after a trio of new desktop publishing technologies—the Apple Macintosh computer, the Hewlett-Packard Laserjet printer, and Aldus PageMaker—were introduced. Many upgrades on these original technologies have improved the technical quality of the countless news and information pieces that have been issued around the world from these new "presses." And the success of some desktop journalists in attracting considerable public attention with their stories has been heartening to those interested in shaking up the news business.

Beyond desktop technologies, the fax machine has also attracted the attention of journalists. Communication via facsimile started in 1842 when Alexander Bain, a Scottish clockmaker, used clock mechanisms to transfer an image from one sheet of electrically conductive paper to another. Eventually, telephone lines were adopted for use in delivering facsimiles, and newspapers began experimenting with fax newspapers in the 1920s and 1930s. In 1924, for example, a facsimile machine was used to send pictures for publication in the newspapers from political conventions in Cleveland and Chicago to New York City. These ventures did not flourish, but in the late 1980s, in line with the recent appearance of facsimile machines in America's workplaces, fax papers were revived through the targeting of businesspeople, travelers, and residents in places so remote that they could not receive daily newspapers. By the mid-1990s, however, fax papers had not gained enough attention from news readers to remain economically viable.

Teletext is a one-way information retrieval service provided to television customers who purchase or rent decoding machines. The BBC began experimenting with teletext in the 1970s by offering text-based information, including national and international news, travel reports, weather reports, and television schedules. Teletext grew in popularity in Great Britain, and television owners in other countries started their own services. Teletext appeared for the first time in the United States in 1978 when the CBS television network tested its new service in St. Louis. Not long after, CBS premiered the service on station KNXT (now KCBS) in Los Angeles, and also in 1978, television station KSL in Salt Lake City started offering the same. Unlike the experience in Great Britain and Europe, however, teletext was not a success in America.

Videotex is similar to teletext in that both require televisions and decoders. These technologies differ, however, in an important way: videotex is a two-way communication process, whereas teletext operators cannot receive signals from their customers. Videotex was under development in the late 1960s when the BBC began to search for ways to send closed-captioning information to audiences. Although several videotex enterprises were launched in the United States in the mid-1980s, Americans did not adopt the technology in large enough numbers for it to become successful.

Audiotex is another recent technology that delivers news and other informational messages. First used by telephone companies for the transmission of time and temperature data, audiotex was eventually employed by news organizations to distribute headline news. Cell phones are currently being used by the operators of the wireless World Wide Web for the delivery of audiotex news messages, and not long ago, cell-phone users started capturing images of breaking news events with their camera phones and videophones. In 2005, a group of citizens turned journalists employed their phones to report on Hurricane Katrina and terrorist bombings in London. World Wide Web–based organizations, such as NowPublic and Flickr, have enabled cell- and videophone journalists to publish their photographs and written stories.

Mainstream journalists began operating bulletin board systems (BBS) for dissemination of news after they started growing in popularity in the 1980s. In 1994, the *Salt Lake Tribune* started a bulletin board newspaper titled *Utah Online*. (They kept this title for their online newspaper edition.) One source maintains that there were about sixty bulletin boards started by newspapers in the short history of this practice.[217]

Designed for the exchange of electronic messages, the first computerized bulletin board went up in 1978 in the suburban

Chicago home of Ward Christensen. He and his friend Randy Suess ran the first BBS on an S-100 computer with 64K RAM. Eventually, bulletin boards became so popular that thousands of forums and special interest groups developed; at their height in the mid-1990s, tens of thousands of bulletin boards operated in the United States. But by the late 1990s, bulletin board memberships had declined sharply as the graphics-oriented World Wide Web began to divert people's attention.

By the mid-1990s, journalists were fully engaged in predicting future new media possibilities. The signs pointed to digital electronics, defined as the conversion of information, sound, video, text, and images into a single code that can be decoded at the other end of the transmission. Huge computer conglomerates were rushing to lead the way. Fiber-optic telephone lines, it was thought, would soon connect everyone to high-definition television, interactive services, and image processing. Within that context, the Internet became the next addition to the journalists' arsenal of tools.

The earliest known descriptions of computer networking were in a series of memos written in 1962 by J. C. R. Licklider of the Massachusetts Institute of Technology (MIT). Calling it his "Galactic Network" concept, Licklider imagined a globally interconnected set of computers through which everyone could quickly access data and programs from any site. Today's Internet is very much like the network he envisioned. The earliest uses of the Internet were noncommercial in nature, but by the early 1980s, a few commercial vendors were learning about networking.

In the 1980s, a handful of papers and broadcasters started dial-up bulletin board systems on the Internet, usually the pet projects of engineers, newsroom technophiles, and marketing departments. Most were partnerships with budding dial-up platforms such as America Online, Prodigy, and CompuServe. Standard fare

on these plain-text services included classifieds, business and entertainment listings, and a few news headlines.

In 1991, the Chicago Tribune Company invested in America
Online. A year later, it launched Chicago Online on AOL with
a sampling of *Chicago Tribune* stories and other newspaper content. Since the early 1990s, publishers of many print newspapers
have established themselves on the Web, although not always
with enthusiasm. The first online newspapers were basically digital versions of printed newspapers. Since one of the advantages
of the Web is that paper is not used, editors quickly realized they
could employ their online editions as a place for material that
would not fit in their regular editions. Over time, newspapers
editors began experimenting with design as they added hypertext and links.

Because reading online newspaper stories is often frustrating
and unfulfilling, online publishers have not seen much growth in
readership. People who love the routine of sitting down with coffee and the paper have not wanted to give up this experience. Online news story's "pages" are hard to read, and though most Web
sites display photos and other graphics, those used are often small.
In response, newspaper publishers have searched for ways to continue publishing on the Web but increase readership at the same
time. Some have offered their customers compact disc (CD) versions of their newspapers.

Today, most newspapers and many broadcast news organizations have invested in the World Wide Web. Not all agree that the
Web is a panacea, but some have asserted that the power of the Internet is awesome. According to the authors of a paper titled "A
Brief History of the Internet," this new technology has "revolu-
tionized the computer world like nothing before. . . . The Internet is at once a world-wide broadcasting capability, a mechanism

for information dissemination, and a medium for collaboration and interaction between individuals and their computers without regard for geographic location."[218]

E-mail became one of the Internet's first gifts to the field of journalism. Since the mid-1990s, the ability to transmit mail electronically has greatly aided reporters and editors in their news-gathering and fact-checking activities. More recently, the Weblog became a second Internet application to be reckoned with by professional journalists. *Merriam-Webster's Dictionary* defines a *Weblog* as a Web site that contains an online personal journal with reflections, comments, and, often, hypertext links selected by the writer. A few years after free Blogger software became available in 1999, the number of Weblogs exploded. According to Technocrati, an online Web-tracking organization, since October 2004, the number of Weblogs has almost doubled to a total of 7.8 million, and between 2004 and 2006, the blogosphere increased to sixteen times its original size.

Weblogs have been put to many uses by news writers in the short history of the phenomenon. In addition to being useful for news dissemination, the Weblog is interactive, which allows for an interchange between publisher and reader that is impossible in traditional news forms. While the main agenda of some bloggers is to cover the news, others are not concerned as much with news as they are with discussion. Since bloggers began publishing news sites, mainstream journalists have engaged in a lively debate about whether they can be considered "real" journalists.

In addition to worrying about the bottom line, print journalists are also concerned about the phenomenon of the blogging journalist. Bloggers write about everything from the ordinary to the profound in their spare time or at work, and some of them claim to be journalists—a contention that has sparked debate. In a book on digital journalism, teacher and technology consultant Kevin Kawamoto started by posing a crucial question: "In this age of digital media, where allegedly anyone can be a publisher, the designation of journalist is increasingly being called into question. Who qualifies for press credentials? Who (or what) is the press in the twenty-first century?"[219]

Journalists have not been in favor of excluding writers from the craft because to do such would violate the spirit of the First Amendment. Unlike law and medicine, journalism is not a licensed profession, meaning anyone with journalistic talent can be admitted to the fold. Most professional journalists, however, pay their dues by getting trained at one of the nation's hundreds of schools of journalism. Once hired, they follow well-defined rules in terms of how to write and report stories, join professional associations, and abide by the canons of journalism. Journalists who break the field's rules run the risk of being fired. In the 1980s, Janet Cooke lost her Pulitzer and her job for lying in her *Washington Post* "Jimmy's World" story. More recently, the dishonored Stephen Glass of the *New Republic,* Jayson Blair of the *New York Times,* and Patricia Smith of the *Boston Globe* caused further embarrassment among defenders of the press.

This dispute fits a common pattern: the emergence of new technologies in the field of journalism has often led to arguments over who ought to be in control of the process of disseminating news and editorial opinion. Debates over control of the news erupted in the 1920s and 1930s between newspaper and radio journalists. More recently, in his bid for the presidency in the early 1990s, Ross Perot organized a series of electronic town meetings that became popular enough that complaints were voiced about how they were eliminating the need for journalists.[220] As a columnist in the *Christian Science Monitor* stated, the

Perot campaign's political strategy was "to get the conventional press out of the way, to cut out the middleman in delivering their messages."[221] Occupational sociologist Andrew Abbott claimed such arguments can be read as signs that a realignment of an occupation's or profession's social boundaries is under way. He recommended that anyone interested in the future of a particular professional group should pay attention to such technology-led battles, since "just as technology creates jurisdictions, so also it destroys them."[222]

For bloggers, the answer to the question of whether they are journalists is easy: of course they're journalists, although that doesn't necessarily mean they want to be confused with mainstream journalism. In a National Public Radio (NPR) interview on the role of Weblogs after the tsunamis of 2004, blogger Xeni Jardin stated: "Bloggers aren't just fat blowhards sitting on couches in the suburbs talking about what they saw on the news. I mean, bloggers are also, like, these [other] journalists in Southeast Asia."[223]

But few nonblogging journalists would agree that bloggers are "real" journalists, as is obvious in the following quotes:

> Bloggers aren't necessarily journalists. And journalists shouldn't be bloggers.[224]

> Most bloggers don't pretend to be journalists. They rarely do original reporting, instead offering observations and opinion.[225]

> The vast majority of blogs are personal and many of those with pretension to journalism are nothing more than rants wrapped around a few facts dredged from the mainstream (and not-so-mainstream) press.[226]

> [Bloggers] are certainly not committed to being objective. They thrive on rumor and innuendo . . . [and] should be put in a different category, like "pretend" journalists.[227]

The last of these statements captures a prominent theme in current commentary on this topic: although bloggers aren't true journalists, they're doing something that resembles journalism. Bloggers have been called by various names, among them pretend journalists, amateur journalists, armchair journalists, parajournalists, and citizen journalists. Others less critical of their role contextualize blogging in the broader history of alternative journalism. Geneva Overholser, who was interviewed for a *Pittsburgh Post-Gazette* piece written in response to the resignation of Dan Rather, said: "The old mainstream media are not all that they once were in terms of being the gatekeepers. CBS put the memos online, to their credit, and all these bloggers within hours found all kinds of questions about the authenticity of the documents. I think that's very reassuring in one sense because it really is the democratization of the media."[228]

Many speak of the lessons traditional journalists ought to be learning as they contend with the impact of blogging on their craft. In the words of Fred Brown of the *Denver Post*:

> One lesson good journalists should take away from this train wreck [referring to Dan Rather's resignation] is that there is no longer any place to hide when you mess up. Weblogs and all the other media that flood the cyberworld with information will pounce on any mistake. They'll be on it like hairspray on an anchorman. In the larger picture, this is a good thing [since] this instantaneous scrutiny forces journalists, especially the high-profile ones, to be accurate and accountable. Still this "gotcha" coup

doesn't mean bloggers suddenly have been raised to the level of mainstream media on the credibility meter.[229]

Although Jay Rosen, publisher of a blog titled *Press Think,* claimed in a January 15, 2005, column that the debate over whether bloggers are journalists is over, he added: "I have been an observer and critic of the American press for 19 years. In that stretch there has never been a time so unsettled. More is up for grabs than has ever been up for grabs since I started my watch." Another question that remains unclear is whether mainstream news organizations will begin to accept bloggers more uniformly among their own ranks. Some journalists who started blogs have been fired. Steve Olafson was fired from his *Houston Chronicle* reporting job in July 2002 when one of his colleagues exposed him as the publisher of a blog that featured disparaging remarks about local politicians. Writing under the pseudonym Banjo Jones, Olafson used his site to lampoon the politicians he covered on his beat.

News media companies argue they may be opening themselves up to questions of liability when their employees set up Weblogs, whether on their personal sites or those of their employers. Jane E. Kirtley, a professor of media ethics and law at the University of Minnesota, said: "If I'm a lawyer advising a news organization, the idea of a Web log like this would just make me break out in hives."[230]

Particularly problematic for news organizations are anonymous blog posts and posts that could result in defamation suits. Legal experts maintain that if a Minnesota defamation suit filed in January 2006 by a Democratic Party public relations consultant against an anonymous Republican blogger goes to trial, it has the potential of becoming a key test of the First Amendment rights of bloggers. The plaintiff in the suit, Blois Olson, claims he was libeled by

Michael Brodkorb in a December 28, 2005, blog posting that suggested he had publicly criticized former Federal Bureau of Investigation (FBI) agent Coleen Rowley's campaign for Congress because Rowley's campaign staff refused to hire his firm, New School Communications. Olson insists the information was fabricated, while Brodkorb insists it is factual.[231] In response to reporter Patrick Sweeney's question about the potential impact of this case, Kirtley said: "The central question here is whether a court is going to treat a blog as being the equivalent of a news organization."[232] She added that the few appellate courts that have ruled on cases involving blogs have generally been lenient in their treatment of them because the public does not expect them to be based entirely on fact.

News organizations worry about the legal problems they could face if they enter the blogosphere; and at the same time, they also fear their image is being marred by its association with bloggers. Professional journalist Jeff Jarvis said blogging is healthy for mainstream journalism because it provides an opportunity to "innovate . . . experiment, [and] try new things." On the question of whether a news organization's reputation could be damaged through its associations with bloggers, he added: "There's a concern that blogs hurt the mainstream brand or divert resources from important journalistic work. The question of the brand is up to our bosses. But I would argue that some of the most important journalistic work we can do is to figure out new ways to gather information, interact with the public and tell stories. And blogging is good for that."[233]

Instead of firing blogging employees, more and more news organizations have added blogs to the online editions of their publications. Dan Gillmor, who produced a blog for the *San Jose Mercury News* from 1999 to 2004, was given free rein by his editors.

Other newspapers tend to be more cautious in their handling of blogs. Late in 2005, as the *New York Times* prepared to launch a new entertainment blog named *Carpetbagger,* editor Jon Landman warned his staff to not give bloggers special treatment. He stated: "Blogs make some newspaper people nuts; they're partisan, the thinking goes, and unfair and mean-spirited and sloppy about facts. Newspapers make some bloggers nuts; they think we're dull and slow and pompous and jealous guardians of unearned authority. ... We'll encourage readers to post their thoughts, but we'll screen them first to make sure the conversation is civil. Some bloggers will accuse us of violating blogospheric standards of openness and spontaneity. That's life in the big city."[234]

Like newspapers, the television news establishment is moving into the blogosphere. One of the leaders in this trend is MSNBC, a twenty-four-hour news cable channel launched in 1996 by the owners of NBC and Microsoft. The channel's online site, MSNBC.com, is currently one of America's most popular providers of news on the Web. In 2002, the site operated seven blogs; by early 2006, the number had grown to twenty-one. The editor of one of MSNBC's blogs, *Get Clicked,* explained his blog's purpose in this comment: "The modern news consumer ignores Weblogs and online citizen journalism at his own peril. But not everyone has the time to keep track of what's going on on the Web. With this blog we hope to track the highlights of what's being discussed online so when news breaks from the Web, we're ready."[235]

As mainstream journalism continues to adjust to the blosphere, it is also dealing with podcasting, another innovative technology with news potential. Its quick adoption by broadcasters and newspapers offers evidence that mainstream journalists are realizing that their fortunes may rest on whether they are willing to embrace multimedia news formats. The word *podcast* only came into use in mid-2004, but by the end of 2005, it had become the *Oxford American Dictionary's* new word of the year. A podcast is an Internet audio or video program that is available to people when and how they want it on their personal computers and/or mobile devices. Audiences can listen to podcasts any time they wish by downloading them over the Internet for use offline or through a portable device. Podcasters distribute their audio and video files over the Internet with either RSS or Atom syndication for use on mobile devices and personal computers. RSS stands for Really Simple Syndication, an XML-based Web syndication tool for Web sites and blogs.

Although they have been used most heavily for music and other entertainment content, podcasts are also being adopted by news organizations. Traditional broadcasters have been eager to pick up on the podcasting format, especially those with predominately news and/or talk show formats. In September 2004, the American syndicated radio show *Web Talk Radio* was one of the first to adopt the podcast as a regular feature.

On May 16, 2005, Infinity Broadcasting, Viacom's radio division, started the world's first all-podcast radio station in San Francisco. Rather than offering downloadable programming, the station is an experiment in "open-source radio." Operators of open-source radio stations ask listeners to produce and upload content they want added to the station's schedule. Infinity Broadcasting's chief executive officer Joel Hollander said: "I'm excited. We're creating a new way to let a lot of people participate personally in radio—sharing their feelings on music, news, politics, whatever matters to them. I think this is going to be a really interesting way to develop new talent."[236]

Television has not been far behind. For instance, ABC began

offering the public a weekly fifteen-minute podcast titled *ABC News Shuffle* in mid-2005. By early 2006, local television stations such as WCPO-TV, the ABC affiliate in Cincinnati, Ohio, and KXAN-TV, NBC's affiliate in Austin, Texas, were also distributing podcasts.

Similarly, newspapers have started podcasting. In early 2006, the *New York Times* launched a series of free podcasts available via the Web's iTunes Music Store, Yahoo! Podcasts, My Yahoo!, and NYTimes.com. Called *New York Times Front Page,* the podcasts were among iTunes's top picks. Vivian Schiller, senior vice president of the *Times*'s television and video division, said: "This is just one of the ways we're expanding *New York Times* journalism into various forms of multimedia as we grow to meet the needs of our audience. Audio and video are natural extensions of our reporting and our brand."[237]

This trend toward increased use of podcasting and other emerging technologies is the future, wrote Joe Strupp in a March 23, 2006, column in *Editor & Publisher.*[238] Strupp's piece, titled "Mixing, Matching, and Multimedia," described what some newspapers are doing today with stories that would have only been disseminated in print fifteen years ago. He wrote: "When The New York Times ran Kurt Eichenwald's Dec. 19 story about a 13-year-old who used his computer to sell sex acts over the Internet, the paper not only ran the piece on its Web site, it also included a Web-only essay and a video interview with the boy. One month later on the opposite coast, Kevin Fagan of the *San Francisco Chronicle* served as a media witness at an execution, then recorded a podcast of his observations before he even began to write his story."

One of Strupp's sources commented that journalists who use multimedia formats to report the news have more impact than they could using one medium only. "Mixing and matching media has a certain impact of its own," said Phil Bronstein, a *San Francisco Chronicle* editor.[239] Since 2005, a growing number of newspapers have reorganized their news departments by integrating their online and print staffs. In addition to the *Times* and *Chronicle,* newspapers such as *USA Today,* the *Sacramento Bee,* and the *Chicago Tribune* have taken such steps in an effort to remain relevant in the field of journalism.

Not everyone in today's news community is as enthusiastic about the potential of multimedia news forms to help extant news institutions better serve the public. Concerns about quality and overworked staff are heard from critics of the trend toward multimedia news distribution. If consumers start to access multimedia news forms, traditional news organizations will continue to move toward convergence. But as Peter Schumacher, a writer for *Online Journalism Review,* explained: "Interactive multimedia features can be challenging for users: Where do I have to click? How do I stop and restart this animation? What navigation options do I have? Multimedia content producers should take a look at their work from a user's perspective."[240] Whether producers of multimedia news pay enough attention to the needs of the public will be key in the future success of such endeavors.

◇

NINE

PRESS AS SYMBOL

That the early American printing press has assumed the stature of a powerful popular icon is clear. Old presses are found in museum exhibits all over the world. Images of printing presses are published on postcards and commemorative postage stamps. And living history programs at historical sites such as such as Colonial Williamsburg have included old printing presses in their public events.[241]

How did the early American printing press come to occupy such a hallowed place in popular culture? Its stature can be attributed, in part, to the fact that from the time of Gutenberg in the fifteenth century, the press's association with dramatic and historical events has precipitated commentary on its perceived power. In sixteenth-century England, Francis Bacon observed: "Printing, gunpowder, and the magnet. . . . these three have changed the whole face and state of things throughout the world." In 1853, Henry David Thoreau wrote: "How often we read that the enemy occupied a position which commanded the old, and so the fort was evacuated! Have not the school-house and the printing-press occupied a position which commands such a fort as this?" And in 1943, American screenwriter Dudley Nichols, in the World

War II movie *This Land Is Mine,* commented on the press in a line written for the mayor of a Nazi-occupied town: "Break up the printing presses and you break up rebellion."[242]

While messages such as these helped elevate the reputation of the printing press, there were other contributing factors as well. Stories about the trials and tribulations of particularly notorious printing presses have been told and retold in popular media over the centuries since the first machine reached Cambridge in 1639. A notable example appeared in a 1939 pamphlet written by Sidney A. Kimber to commemorate the arrival of the Cambridge press three hundred years earlier. Kimber began his *Story of an Old Press* with these words: "Less than a score of years after the Pilgrims moored their bark at Plymouth in 1620, there was established at Cambridge the first printing press in the English colonies in North America."[243]

The rest of Kimber's account identified the individuals who carried the press to North America, why they embarked on such a journey, where their press was first set up, who operated it, and what was printed on it. From there, Kimber recounted how, sometime after 1765, printer Bartholomew Green took the press to Boston, where it was "perhaps used . . . in printing *The News Letter* in 1704."[244] Fifty years later, the press was transported to New London, Connecticut, and between 1778 and 1779, to Dresden, Vermont, and then Westminster, Vermont, where the state's first newspaper was published in 1781.

Thus associated with not only North America's but also Vermont's first newspaper, the pedigree of the press was firmly established. This led to the publication of other works that have told its story. Moreover, it appeared on a U.S. Postal Service commemorative stamp in 1939, and it was placed on display at the museum of the Vermont Historical Society, in Montpelier.[245]

Stories that focus on the life histories of American printing presses have circulated widely in popular culture. Some of these stories were the main topic of stand-alone pamphlets, newspaper and magazine articles, and even books. Others were found in more general press-related material in American, state, and local press histories and in autobiographies or biographies of early printers. A third group of stories are available on Web sites, as well as in history museum exhibits and living history demonstrations.

One of the most prevalent themes embedded within stories about printing presses and those who operated them relates to the great American value of perseverance. According to the stories, printers were a tough and tenacious breed whose mettle was tested in dangerous journeys across the ocean and later on the harsh American frontier. Along with this hardy lot came printing presses, which provided fodder for many tales about the experiences of settlers. Some of the more common stories on America's early printing presses were those that told how a territory's or state's first press made its way to a remote destination on the frontier. In fact, people in every state of the nation have published at least one history of the state's newspaper press, and often, such accounts start with tales that describe the lengths to which the early press operators went to get their presses to the far reaches of the frontier.

The oldest of these presses was the British colony's first printing press. Called the Daye press and, alternatively, the Cambridge press, it arrived on the shores of New England in the summer of 1638 on a ship named the *John of London*. According to press historian Robert F. Roden, the ship's arrival ended "one of the most memorable of voyages." On its trip across the Atlantic, its owner, Joseph Glover, "fell sick of a feaver and dyed." After landing, the establishment of the press was carried on by Glover's widow,

Elizabeth Harris, who set up a printing house and arranged for the publication of its first imprint.[246]

The press's journey, the death of its owner, and the events that transpired after its arrival at Cambridge were likely considered important news both in New England and back home at London. At that time in the colonies, news was circulated largely by word of mouth and in letters, pamphlets, and books because no newspapers had yet been established. Nevertheless, several accounts of the press's journey and establishment at Cambridge were soon forthcoming. The first was a letter written after the press arrived at Cambridge by Salem teacher Hugh Peters, sent to a Virginia minister who was off preaching in Bermuda. Peters's letter began: "Wee have a printery here and thinke to goe to worke with some speciall things, and if you have any thing you may send it safely." A story of what happened to the press and its owner was circulated to a wider audience in a book titled *History of New-England,* published in 1654. These accounts of the press's arrival were followed by the Kimber and Roden printing press stories. In addition, Isaiah Thomas included an account of the Daye press's arrival and history at Cambridge in his famous history of America's printing.[247]

Considering the distance that separated the California territory from the rest of the United States, accounts of the way in which the owners of its earliest printing presses got them there have been the source for some colorful storytelling. In 1934, Carl I. Wheat's *Pioneers: The Engaging Tale of Three Early California Printing Presses and Their Strange Adventures* was published.[248] Its author told how California's first press was ordered in 1829 from Boston by a young man named Agustin V. Zamorano, recently arrived in Monterey from Mexico City. The press, which cost Zamorano $460 including delivery, was an old Ramage machine—"a weather-beatin relic even then, purchased no doubt from some fourth-rate New England print shop."[249] The cross-country journey would take several years, and after only a short stay at Monterey, the press was taken to Sonoma by General Mariano Guadelupe Vallejo. After a brief sojourn at Sonoma, it was taken back to Monterey, where it was used for a time but eventually "junked" in a deserted adobe.[250]

In July 1846, the Zamorano press was rediscovered by Rev. Walter Colton, author, lecturer, preacher, and chaplain of the USS *Congress*. Appointed to a position of authority in Monterey, Colton got the itch to print. He teamed up with Robert Semple, a buckskin-clad frontiersman, to find a press. Hearing that one had operated in the 1830s at Monterey, the two searched until they found the old Ramage. After repairing its ink-balls, scouring its type, oiling its joints, and setting it up, the pair gave the world the first issue of a newspaper called the *Californian*.[251]

Five years later, Semple took the press via boat to Yerba Buena, a little settlement on the western shore of San Francisco Bay. Remaining there a short time, it was moved, via its cast of ever-changing owners, to Benicia, Sacramento, Stockton, Sonora, and finally Columbia, where it met its ultimate fate. When the press's last owner could not make his payments, the machine was taken from its shop to an adjacent sidewalk. That night, a group of ruffians dragged the old Ramage to the middle of the street and set it on fire. In a few minutes, it was gone. As one author put it: "even in a barbarian country" such a press would "have been held in veneration a life time, if only as an unmeaning curiosity." In other words, a press with such a long history of perseverance deserved a better end.[252]

Wheat was moved to tell another story of perseverance in his account of California's early printing presses and their "strange adventures." This press was called the Old Ames Press, and it was taken to California in 1850 by Judge John Judson Ames. A passage from Wheat's pamphlet relates its journey:

What a story that old press could tell! It has been said, though the tale is perhaps apocryphal, that it was first bought in New York in 1848, and taken to Baton Rouge, home of General Zachary Taylor, where—it is related—Ames printed on it "The Dime Catcher," A Whig organ puffing Taylor for the Presidency. Be that as it may, we find Ames struggling with it on the Isthmus [Panama] in the Chagres River wherein it had fallen from a native canoe. At Gorgona it was taken to pieces and loaded on the backs of several Isthmian mules, and at least Ames reached Panama, there—while awaiting transportation to California—to print The Panama Herald, organ of the horde of stranded Argonauts on that fever-laden shore.[253]

Eventually, the Old Ames Press made it to California, where Ames headed for Sacramento and became connected with the *Placer Times and Transcript*. Later, Ames took it to San Diego, where he established that new town's first newspaper, and still later to San Bernardino. Then, under new ownership, the press was taken in 1862 over the Cajon Pass, across the Mojave Desert, and up to a town named Aurora through the Owens Valley and along the eastern flank of the Sierra in what would become Nevada. In 1870, the press returned to Fort Independence, California, where it printed the first issue of the *Inyo Independent*. After that, it fell into disuse, but through letters and other communication, Henry Ford, in Michigan, heard of the press and moved it to his museum, where it was placed on display. As one author put it: "Now the old press rests in peace after its years of labor. Perchance the time may come when some famed printer may again pull on its aged drawbar, and impress with the old-time type on old-time paper the tale of its eventful life."[254]

Another theme within stories of old printing presses relates to the cause of freedom. Since the American Revolution, stories have proliferated about printing presses that were threatened or destroyed as their owners defended their right to operate them. Through the telling of such stories, the printing press is linked to a value central to American democratic culture: namely, the virtue of valor in the face of those who seek to deprive citizens of their freedom. An example from the era of the American Revolution is the story of how a press the British called a "sedition factory" escaped destruction in 1775. The story is told, among other places, in a pamphlet titled *Old "No. 1": The Story of Isaiah Thomas and His Printing Press.*[255] Thomas's work for Boston's Sons of Liberty put both him and his press in harm's way. He had used his press to print the first reports of the battles of Lexington and Concord with the bold headline AMERICANS!!—LIBERTY OR DEATH!—JOIN OR DIE!!

For this, the authorities sought revenge, and Thomas was forced to dismantle and move his press across the Charles River to safety. Not long after, it was moved to the town of Worcester, some forty miles west, where it would continue to provoke the British. Thomas came to so treasure his press that he decided to preserve it for posterity. Eventually, he helped establish the American Antiquarian Society, one of the nation's premier libraries of early American history. Old No. 1 is still on display in the halls of the society's Worcester facility.

Both Thomas and his press had long and productive lives, but others weren't as lucky. In 1837, newspaper editor and abolitionist Elijah P. Lovejoy was murdered in Alton, Illinois, by a mob furious over his refusal to stop printing antislavery editorials. Before his murder, the mobs destroyed several of Lovejoy's printing presses by smashing them to bits and throwing them into the Mississippi River.[256]

The story of Lovejoy's murder by the friends of slavery has been told over and over, and of course, the emphasis has been on the horror of his death. But also in these accounts are detailed descriptions of the destruction of his printing presses. Shortly after he was killed, a November 7, 1837, article published in *the Alton Observer* described what happened. Based on this article, a Web site devoted to memorializing Lovejoy provides this summary of what happened the night he died:

> Night had come to the town of Alton, Illinois and a crowd began to gather in the darkness. Some of the men stooped to gather stones. Others fingered the triggers of the guns they carried as they made their way to a warehouse on the banks of the Mississippi River. As they approached, they eyed the windows of the three-story building, searching for some sign of movement from inside. Suddenly, William S. Gilman, one of the owners of the building, appeared in an upper window. "What do you want here?" he asked the crowd. "The press!" came the shouted reply. Inside the warehouse was Elijah Parish Lovejoy, a Presbyterian minister and editor of the *Alton Observer.* He and 20 of his supporters were standing guard over a newly arrived printing press from the Ohio Anti-Slavery Society. This was the fourth press that Lovejoy had received for his paper. Three others already had been destroyed by people who opposed the antislavery views he expressed in the *Observer.* But Lovejoy would not give up.[257]

The metal part from a printing press believed to have been one of Lovejoy's was discovered in the 1850s in the Mississippi River near Alton. What remains of the press has been placed on exhibit in the lobby of the *Telegraph* newspaper at Alton.[258] Accounts of what happened to Lovejoy and his presses are told in other museum exhibits, as well as in books, pamphlets, and Web sites.

Lovejoy's presses weren't the only ones destroyed by mobs inflamed over the issue of slavery. When abolitionist editor and orator Jane Grey Swisshelm moved to the Minnesota frontier in 1850, her printing press was thrown into a river after she refused to succumb to the threats of a mob that demanded that she stop printing antislavery material. The fate of Swisshelm and her printing press has been told in numerous published works.[259] Beyond that, the Minnesota Historical Society has retold the story in a living history theater presentation at its St. Paul museum.

Further violence directed toward printing presses occurred in the Bleeding Kansas era and later during the Civil War. The Kansas State Historical Society's collections include type from the printing press that published the city of Lawrence's *Herald of Freedom*. The story of what happened to the press, which was thrown into the street during an 1856 raid that destroyed its office, is told in publications such as Richard Cordley's history of Lawrence.[260] The bed from a press that printed another Lawrence newspaper, the *Tribune,* was salvaged as a Civil War relic after border ruffian William Quantrill sacked the city in 1863 in the strife that engulfed the community over the extension of slavery. And in 1857, a rumor that a printing press was destroyed began to circulate after the town of Osawatomie, in Miami County, was sacked by proslavery men. According to one correspondent, however, this was a false rumor. John Everett, who had read the statements about the Osawatomie raid published in eastern papers, wrote on June 27, 1856: "Our printing office was not destroyed as reported I see in the Eastern papers. It was buried in the ground and they could not find it."[261]

Stories about the printing presses used to spread Christianity through missionaries to Native Americans or other groups linked them to another core American value—the importance of religion, particularly Christianity. Such was the case with printer and religious proselytizer Jotham Meeker, born in Ohio in 1804 and trained as a printer at Cincinnati. As told by press historian Douglas C. McMurtrie and other writers, Meeker's place in the history of the printing press was established by the fact that he was the first printer in Kansas Territory.[262] At age twenty-one, after he decided to become a missionary to the Indians of the Michigan Territory, Meeker was assigned to teach among the Pottawatomis, Ottawas, and Chippewas. While in Michigan, he learned to speak three Native American languages and began experimenting with a phonetic system of Indian orthography. Using ordinary English type, he began printing material in the languages of Indian people.

The Board of Baptist Missions sent Meeker to Kansas in 1833. The U.S. government had ordered eastern Indian tribes to lands west of the Missouri River, where more than twenty nations were promised possession "so long as the sun shone, the grass grew and the rivers ran downhill." Meeker was assigned to the Shawnee tribe as a printer-missionary. He set out with his wife and a printing press in September 1833. He moved the press from Ohio by boat to Independence, Missouri, and by wagon to the mission. His expense account listed the following: "Printing apparatus, including transportation, $468.13. . . . In the article of printing apparatus, I include $35.00 worth of paper and ink."[263]

By February 1834, Meeker had set up his press at the Shawnee Baptist Mission in present-day Johnson County, Kansas. The following month, his first work appeared, a twenty-four-page primer in the Delaware language. In all, he printed some sixty-five works in ten Indian languages, including a newspaper, the *Shawnee Sun*. Most of Meeker's work was of a religious nature, and all of it used his phonetic system of printing. When he died in 1855, his influence among the Indians was evidenced in an obituary notice printed in the *Missionary Magazine:* "His probity and his interested concern won the most confiding affection of the people. They looked up to him as a father and consulted him on all national concerns; and so single was their trust in him, that they would not receive their money from the government till he had first counted it."[264]

The ingenuity of Americans has been the stuff of legends, and so have some printing presses and their operators. Thus it was with "the Press on Wheels," whose story has been preserved since it operated on America's high plains in the days of the frontier. This press followed the Union Pacific Railroad as it expanded westward through Wyoming. Pioneer publisher Legh (often spelled Leigh) Richmond Freeman wrote that it would "require a volume larger than Webster's unabridged dictionary to touch on anything like the most interesting incidents that have transpired on the camping grounds of this press."[265]

Freeman is regarded as a pioneer journalist in the Rocky Mountain region. He and his wife and occasionally his brother, Richmond, published an itinerant newspaper, the *Frontier-Index*. In 1943, printing historian Douglas McMurtrie pieced together the story of Freeman's newspapers using existing issues and contemporary sources. McMurtrie started with a Freeman quote taken from a July 26, 1867, newspaper issued at Julesburg, Colorado: "[While the] Union Pacific was building westward, our 'press on wheels' was publishing in all its terminal towns. One day it printed the outside of the paper in North Platte City, dating it Julesburg, then the outfit was put aboard one of the cars and after being transported 100 miles, was set out on the greensward of the unbroken prairie, a set of tarpaulins stretched over, the locals rustled up, and Julesburg had her paper the same day that the outside had been printed a hundred miles away."[266]

Freeman further recounted that his "office" was drawn across the Rocky Mountains on the first construction train that crossed them. And McMurtrie's research further documented that

Freeman, as he moved his press from place to place, published papers across the high plains in Cheyenne, Fort Sanders, Laramie, Green River, and Bear River. In his years in the region, Freeman claimed to have "covered thirteen states and territories with our circulation," accompanied by his "Press on Wheels."

Evidence that the printing presses had reached the status of an American icon by the mid-nineteenth century is seen in the various arguments that have surrounded their whereabouts and pedigrees. Two of the disputes arose over the "true" histories of the first presses to arrive in Kansas and Minnesota. Starting with Kansas in 1834, Jotham Meeker set up the first printing press west of the Mississippi, at Shawnee Mission, Kansas, and it remained in operation under the auspices of the Baptist Missionary Society for more than twenty years. In either 1856 or 1857, the society sold it to G. W. Brown, who moved it to Lawrence, Kansas. Brown used the press for a few years to publish a newspaper titled the *Herald of Freedom,* although it is unclear how long he owned it. Rev. John G. Pratt, who, along with Meeker, operated the press for the missionary society, claimed it was "utterly demolished in Quantrel's [*sic*] raid" in 1863. But Pratt's contention does not square with others' stories about what happened to the press. According to one source, the Meeker press was moved in 1857 to Prairie City, Kansas, where it operated for some time. From there, other sources have it being taken to other Kansas locations, including Cottonwood Falls and Winfield.[267]

In the late 1870s, as a group of Kansas editors sought to establish the Kansas State Historical Society, a formal search for the Meeker press began. In July 1877, Franklin G. Adams, first secretary of the society, received a letter from W. H. Kerns of Sedalia, Missouri, who stated that he had owned the "Meeker Printing Press" for two or three years at Winfield, Kansas (Cowley County) before taking it to Sedalia. From there, Kerns said, he sold the press to someone in Windsor, Missouri. "It is the same press thrown in the river at Lawrence by 'Border Ruffians,' and its history is full of interesting items," Kerns wrote to Adams.[268]

Kerns promised to check on the press and get back to Adams. Six months later, Adams sent another letter to Kerns, who replied in February 1878 that the Meeker press was in southeast Missouri and could be purchased for $100. Again, Kerns promised to follow up and, again, a long time passed before he inquired, in January 1883, as to whether the historical society was still interested in the press. He offered to produce the machine in March if the historical society would buy it for $3,000.

When Adams and the historical society balked at this stiff price tag, Kerns brusquely stated that would make no further propositions. "I shall leave the place where it is unknown," he wrote, "and if the Historical Society is too poor to pay anything for it I shall bury its history so deep it will never be straightened out."[269]

Another angle on the mystery started in northeast Kansas, when a letter in the *Atchison Champion* in June 1878 reported the sighting of the press in Oxford, a town in southern Kansas. The letter writer stated that the press was the same one thrown in the Missouri and Marais des Cygne Rivers by proslavery partisans.

Advocates of yet another version of the Meeker press's fate said the machine went to Indian territory, where "the type and other material used at the mission farm by Mr. Meeker was scattered on the prairie by the Indian children, and as late as 1865, handfuls of type could be picked up near where lies buried one of the most zealous missionaries that ever labored in any land."[270]

An additional account of the history of the Meeker press placed it in Dodge City. According to a story printed in the *Topeka Journal* on February 1, 1902, the press ended up in Elmdale, Kansas, where it belonged to Charles Garten, editor of the *Elmdale Reporter,* who used it to print his weekly newspaper. The author of the Topeka paper article also told of the press being thrown out of a second-story window during Quantrill's raid in Lawrence. Years later, the article stated, the press was purchased by Sam M. Wood of Cottonwood Falls, Kansas. From there, it reportedly went to Winfield (Kansas), Kansas City, and Dodge City before landing in Elmdale.

A few years after the discovery of the press in Garten's possession in Elmdale, a Meade man wrote to the secretary of the state historical society, stating that the Meeker press had been found in the office of the *Guymon (Okla.) Herald*. The author of the letter traced the history of the press from Sedalia, Missouri, to Liberal, Kansas, and finally to Oklahoma. Kansas State Historical Society officials authenticated the origin of the press after it was shipped from Guymon to Topeka. The press—after its missing parts were remade of wood and fitted into place—was later put on exhibition and was the subject of a lecture at the Kansas Baptist Convention in Kansas City. The press also was displayed in the state historical museum for several months before it was returned to Guymon.

In research leading up to a 1935 *Kansas Historical Quarterly* article titled "The Mystery of the Meeker Press," Kirke Mechem conducted a thorough investigation of all these various and sundry claims and their documentation. He concluded that it was impossible to solve the mystery over the whereabouts of the Meeker press. He wrote:

> Perhaps it was destroyed in one of the raids on Lawrence [thrown into the Kansas River by border ruffians] or was disposed of in some obscure transaction of which, so far at least, we have no record. Possibly Kerns [W. H. Kerns of Sedalia, Missouri] did take it to Missouri, and it may still be in existence in some country print shop. Certainly the myths relating to its migrations, if

they are old enough to be called myths, are as curious as any in the annals of Kansas—and Kansas history contains some strange myths. But whatever the state does, it does wholeheartedly. Where only seven cities strove for the distinction of being known as Homer's birthplace, Kansas, in the short space of seventy-five years, has furnished ten towns with claims on a press which in all likelihood was never seen in any of them.[271]

Minnesota was the center of another mystery that turned into a dispute over the location of the state's first printing press. In 1849, lawyer and printer James M. Goodhue loaded his press and all its equipment on a steamer and headed to St. Paul, then a young town of about thirty people. On arriving, Goodhue immediately set up a printing office. After a few successful years of publishing the town's newspaper and numerous government publications, he died. His brother Isaac took over his business for several years but sold the paper and press to Earl S. Goodrich in early 1854.

In 1905, the Minnesota Historical Society acquired a press it claimed was the Goodhue press. According to its records, Goodhue had used the press to print the state's first newspaper, the *Minnesota Pioneer*.[272] But over the next few decades, challenges arose from other parties who insisted that the press was an impostor. Various claims asserted Goodhue's original press was either in South Dakota or Wisconsin or was last used in Winnipeg, Canada, where it was destroyed by fire. South Dakota and Minnesota newspapers printed numerous articles on the squabble; indignant letters to the editor came from various historical societies; and scholars and students wrote papers on the whereabouts of Goodhue's press, contradicting each other and often themselves.[273]

In 1999, the Minnesota Historical Society once again raised the question as to whether the press in its collection was really that taken to Minnesota by James M. Goodhue.[274] After looking at all the claims and evidence, the society's historians agreed that it was. In an article published in its quarterly journal, a society historian explained that the most convincing argument against the authenticity of the society's press was based on inaccurate information. Later, the society announced a series of living history dramatic presentations devoted to telling the story of the Goodhue press.

Scholars conceive of storytelling as a communication practice that both constructs and reflects social and cultural values of a group of people or a nation. While a number of stories are told for strictly didactic purposes, some are told for other reasons. Nevertheless, all stories have meaning that goes beyond their descriptive content. According to Hannah Arendt, "Storytelling reveals meaning without committing the error of defining it."[275]

Considering the interesting things that have happened to printing presses, one can see why those with a talent for writing took up their pens. America's printing presses have been subjected to long and arduous journeys, have survived through revolutions and wars, have been used as instruments to spread religion, and have been subjected to intense and sometimes violent social strife. And while the stories that have been told about printing press are often interesting and sometimes even dramatic, they can also be read for what they have contributed to our understanding of the press's social and cultural values. More than quaint tales, stories of presses circulating through popular media have been part of the ongoing social construction of the printing press and journalism's other technologies as tools with connections to such core American values as freedom, perseverance, religion, industriousness, local pride, and competition.

TEN

THE FUTURE OF PRINTED NEWS

In 1854, newspaper publishers had plenty of reasons to be optimistic. That year, Henry David Thoreau wrote: "The newspaper is a Bible which we read every morning and every afternoon, standing and sitting, riding and walking. It is a Bible which every man carries in his pocket, which lies on every table and counter, and which the mail, and thousands of missionaries, are continually dispersing. It is, in short, the only book which America has printed, and which America reads. So wide is its influence."[276] After 1800, the number of newspapers published in America grew from about two hundred to well into the thousands, and in the country's urban centers, circulations of some expanded exponentially. New kinds of newspapers were published for the nation's Native Americans, African Americans, laborers, pacifists, religious organizations, immigrants, and others with concerns or reform agendas unsatisfied by mainstream papers. And while many news publishers still struggled to eke out a living, some were carving out sizable fortunes in their efforts to serve their readers.

Contributing to the improved prospects of those who published the nation's newspapers were social, economic, geographic, political, and cultural transformations that were part of the broader process of change in America. The individuals who had started the penny press papers of the country's urban centers had discovered that if they catered to the interests of their community's working class, they could sell more news. But another important lesson learned by those practicing journalism in the several decades before the American Civil War related to technology: the future of the country's newspapers would depend not only on publishers' advantageous cultivation of contextual conditions such as changes in population and other developments but also on their willingness to experiment with new technologies. Evidence of this was visible in the favorable results of newspaper publishers' investments in the telegraph, lithography, and speedier printing presses. And by the time the newspaper was in its golden age at the turn of the twentieth century, this technological lesson had been demonstrated time and time again through the period when the photographic halftone and electricity were introduced into the business.

But as history so often reminds us, those who reach the pinnacle of success are often plagued by fears of failure, and people in the field of newspaper journalism were no exception. Even at the height of their prosperity, publishers and others involved in the print news business undoubtedly worried about what the future held for them when newspapers suffered setbacks during economic panics or other hard times. But not until the 1920s, when a new form of communication technology—the radio—had begun to encroach so significantly into the domain of the newspaper journalist would the industry erupt in full-blown panic over the question of whether printed news was on the path to extinction. And while the newspaper ultimately survived the threat of radio, two additional technological assaults on the viability of printed news have developed. In the 1950s and 1960s, television's emergence as an especially popular deliverer of news led to a plethora of commentary on whether newspapers would survive the competition. And today, the intrusion of the World Wide Web's news sites and blogs into the field of journalism has once again precipitated nervous discussion about the survival of print.

Just what the future holds for printed news is impossible to know, but history offers us more than a few lessons about the survivability of the medium of printed news within environments in which new technologies and other potential threats have developed. Immediately after the earliest radio stations began broadcasting in 1921, newspaper publishers took note and began to wonder what, if anything, might happen. Then, in 1922, worries about the threat of radio triggered what historians have often referred to as the press-radio war. Concerns about the loss of circulation and advertising dollars led the Associated Press wire service to issue a notice to its subscribers that AP news copy was not to be used for broadcasting purposes. The annoyance felt by newspaper people when confronted with the notion that radio ought to benefit from the tremendous resources of the Associated Press was reflected in a comment printed in a 1931 issue of *Editor & Publisher*: "Newspapers helped build the new plaything of the nation."[277]

The dispute remained largely a cold war until 1933 when the Associated Press and American Newspaper Publishers Association "Declare[d] War on Radio."[278] The AP and ANPA had just announced that their members had ratified a document known as the Biltmore Agreement. During the years preceding the agreement, radio's phenomenal growth had cut into newspaper revenues, and the effects of the Great Depression were being felt. Industry concerns about the future of newspapers had ratcheted up as newspapers that owned radio stations were using the resources of the Associated Press to build the radio news industry. Among other things, the Biltmore Agreement ordered AP newspapers involved in radio news broadcasting to limit their newscasts to occasional unsponsored, thirty-word bulletins. It also stated that members engaged in local broadcasting would be charged additional assessments. Finally, it notified newspapers that they must start treating the radio program logs they regularly published free of charge as advertising matter.

By 1939, print journalists' lack of success in enforcing the agreement led them to give up the war. Over the preceding decade, some had begun forming lucrative links to radio. Some newspapers ran articles designed to help the public become familiar with radio and its capabilities. Some who could afford it purchased their own radio stations. By the mid-1920s, between fifty and one hundred of America's approximately five hundred radio stations were either owned or affiliated with newspapers. Gradually, as their antagonism dissipated, newspaper people deemed it wiser to find ways to somehow make a profit from radio. In the title of an article in its May 1, 1937, issue, *Broadcasting* magazine announced: "Newspapers End Antagonism to Radio." Publishers and editors, it was stated, had started viewing radio as an established institution. The most recent annual meetings of the AP and ANPA were not marred as they had been previously by hostile rhetoric toward radio.

As television captured the attention of the public in the 1950s and 1960s, it had a profound impact not just on newspapers but also on newsmagazines. The nation's popular weekly newsmagazines, such as *Time, Newsweek, Life,* and *Look,* lost advertisers to television. *Collier's* and the *Saturday Evening Post* died as a result of television, and newspapers likewise experienced losses in advertising sales. The time consumers previously spent reading newspapers shifted to television viewing. Evening newspaper circulations began to slide as television rounded out its late-afternoon, evening, and late-night news programs. There were four evening newspapers in New York City in 1950, but that number fell to two and then, by the end of the decade, to just one. The newsreel and radio news program also lost out to television in the 1950s.

Although a great deal of angst was once again expressed by members of the newspaper community over the future of print, the strategies newspaper leaders developed to cope with the widespread use of television news were much different from those adopted in the 1920s and 1930s. Instead of engineering a war against the upstart television news broadcasters, newspaper leaders decided to build on the paper's strengths rather than on its weaknesses. Ironically, in the process, the emergence of the new medium of television led to a number of improvements in newspapers. Newspapers adapted by informing readers in ways that television and radio could not. Readers could pick up and read newspapers anytime they wanted to. Most newspapers were produced in the communities they were published in, so their contents could provide more local news than radio and television could possibly cover in their brief time slots. Newspapers could include long interpretive pieces of news and commentary that were beyond the scope of television and radio news reports providers. Television primarily entertained, whereas newspapers informed. Newspaper publishers also invested in new technologies, such as the use of color and more graphics, in hopes of adding to the appeal of their products.

Recently, the idea that printed newspapers might not survive has taken on new life because of the success of online news forms and new software that enables anyone to start publishing the news. Evidence of people's keen interest in blogs is everywhere. The publishers of the *Merriam-Webster's Dictionary* announced in early

2005 that the word looked up most often during the previous year by users of their online edition was *blog*—a shortened form of *Weblog*.[279] Dubbed by experts as "the year of the blog," 2004 brought an upsurge not only in the public's interest in the phenomenon but also in people's ability to harness its potential.

All this will come as no surprise to anyone following cyberspace's recent history. Since 1999, when Blogger and other simple blogging tools were released, the number of Weblogs on the Internet has grown exponentially. One tracker of the blog phenomenon reported in August 2005 that the blogosphere was sixteen times larger than it had been just a few years earlier. Today, blogs designed for families and friends are very popular, as are those dedicated to any of a seemingly limitless range of topics. Many blogs attempt to keep their readers up to date on the latest news. From political stories to reports on disasters and wars, blogs created within minutes of when an event occurs are attracting the attention of people who traditionally got their news from other sources.

What does this portend for the future of print news? According to some newspaper publishers and editors, possible annihilation lies ahead. Already strained by the loss of ad dollars, the rising price of paper, and lagging circulations, some of these individuals fear the popularity of Weblogs as news venues bodes ill for the future of the newspaper. In a report prepared for the editors of the *Greensboro News-Record,* Lex Alexander, the paper's online editor, warned: "We have very little choice . . . not to move in this direction . . . [since they will annihilate us] within a generation."[280]

Alexander accurately captured the sense of panic among many of today's news publishers, and a quick glance at the history of print journalism demonstrates its perennially vulnerable nature. But in fact, those with their eyes on the future have thought for quite some time that innovation is once again inevitable. In a 1994 seminar on "The Future of Newspapers and the Newspaper of the Future," Arthur Ochs Sulzberger Jr., publisher of the *New York Times,* said:

> When one buys a New York Times, one buys a guide. One buys judgment. One buys talent. One buys credibility. And today, as in years past, one gets a little something special left over with which to wrap the fish. If, in the years ahead, we must give up that something special with which to wrap the fish, well, that's a cost I'm willing to bear. The plain truth is I don't give a tinker's damn how we distribute our information. As long as our customers want it on newsprint, I'll do all I can to give it to them on newsprint. If they want it on CD-ROM, I'll try to meet that need. The Internet? That's fine. Hell, if someone would be kind enough to invent a technology, I'll be pleased to beam it directly into your cortex. We'll have the city edition, the late city edition, and the mind-meld edition.[281]

The mounting expense of printing news on paper, coupled with the increasing viability of the relatively cheap alternative of online news, has brought another threat to print journalists—that of the citizen journalist. The profession of journalism has always been open to anyone who can write and has a nose for news. But the ease with which one can become an online journalist—and the resulting proliferation of news blogs—has provoked a new set of reactions. One self-serving strategy of mainstream print journalists is to seek to recapture the public's confidence by differentiating professional newspeople from citizen journalists. A term coined not long ago, a *citizen journalist* is anyone who contributes news to a news Web site or Weblog, whether he or she has professional training or not. While some papers, such as the *Houston Chronicle,* regularly announce that they welcome citizen journalists, not all are equally as welcoming. Fred Brown titled a piece he published in a 2005 edition of the *Quill* "'Citizen' Journalism Is Not Professional Journalism."[282] Although Brown admitted "there's a lot to be said in favor of blogs," he stressed the importance of recognizing citizen journalism for what it is. He stated: "There is a difference between 'citizen' journalism and 'professional' journalism. A professional journalist's No. 1 obligation is to be accurate. A citizen journalist's No. 1 obligation is to be interesting. A professional journalist has layers of editors checking his facts. A citizen journalist is usually a lone crusader."

History teaches us that news publishers rarely change the way they do business unless they have no other choice. In the face of today's challenges, publishers of printed news have started to adapt, and they will likely continue to do so until the environment becomes more stable. What is impossible to know is just how far such changes will take the field from its past. The good news is, however, that today's emerging technologies have provoked a stimulating and much-needed dialogue about journalism's past, journalism's future, and journalism's practices and standards.

NOTES

PREFACE

1. "Amazing Kaypro," advertisement of the Kaypro Corporation, which was rated the fifth-largest personal computer manufacturer in the world in 1983. Seven years later, after the MS-DOS operating system successfully crowded out Kaypro's CPM operating system, the corporation filed for bankruptcy.

2. Raymond Williams, *Harmful Myths: Television—Technology and Cultural Form* (New York: Oxford, 1978); James W. Carey, with John J. Quirk, "The Mythos of the Electronic Revolution," in Carey, *Communication as Culture: Essays on Media and Society* (Boston: Unwin Hyman, 1989), 113.

CHAPTER ONE

3. Walter Benjamin, "The Work of Art in the Age of Mechanical Reproduction," 1936, section 13, *Cybernetics or Control and Communication in the Animal and the Machine* (Cambridge, Mass.: MIT Press, 1948).

4. Examples include Thomas Francis Carter's *Invention of Printing in China and Its Spread Westward* (New York: Columbia University Press, 1925) and Bradford F. Swan's *Spread of Printing: Western Hemisphere—The Caribbean Area* (Amsterdam: Van Gendt, 1970).

5. Isaiah Thomas, *The History of Printing in America, with a Biography of Printers,* 2d ed. (1810, repr. New York: B. Franklin, 1967).

6. Ibid., 3, 4.

7. Joseph Tinker Buckingham, *Specimens of Newspaper Literature, with Personal Memoirs, Anecdotes, and Reminiscences* (Boston: Ticknor, Reed, and Fields, 1850) and *Personal Memoirs and Recollections of Editorial Life* (Boston: Ticknor, Reed, and Fields, 1852).

8. Fredrick Hudson, *Journalism in the United States, from 1690–1872* (New York: Harper and Brothers, 1873), 43.

9. Joseph Griffin's 1872 book, *History of the Press of Maine* (Brunswick, Me.: Press of J. Griffin), and William Henry Perrin's 1888 monograph, titled *The Pioneer Press of Kentucky* (Louisville, Ky.: Filson Club Publications), are part of this group. See Joseph Atkinson and Thomas Moran, *The History of Newark, New Jersey, Being a Narrative of Its Rise and Progress, from the Settlement in May, 1666, by Emigrants from Connecticut to the Present Time, Including a Sketch of the Press of Newark, from 1791 to 1878* (Newark, N.J.: W. B. Guild, 1878). In 1939, *Frontier Journalism in San Francisco*, volume 2 of *History of Journalism in San Francisco* (San Francisco: History of San Francisco Journalism Project), was published by writers involved in that city's WPA Writers' Program.

10. S. N. D. North, *History and Present Condition of the Newspaper and Periodical Press of the United States, with a Catalogue of the Publications of the Census Year* (Washington, D.C.: Government Printing Office, 1884); William S. Rossiter, *Manufactures: Printing and Publishing* (Washington, D.C.: Bureau of the Census, 1902).

11. Willard G. Bleyer, *Main Currents in the History of American Journalism* (New York: Houghton Mifflin, 1927), iii. See also James Melvin Lee, *History of American Journalism* (Boston and New York: Houghton Mifflin, 1923); Alfred McClung Lee, *The Daily Newspaper in America* (New York: Macmillan, 1937).

12. Bleyer, *Main Currents,* 399.

13. Ibid.

14. Ibid., 390–2.

15. Robert E. Park, "The Natural History of the Newspaper," *American Journal of Sociology* 29 (November 1925): 273–89.

16. Walter Lippmann, "Two Revolutions of the American Press," *Yale Review* 20 (March 1931): 433–41.

17. Frank Luther Mott, *American Journalism* (New York: Macmillan, 1941).

18. William David Sloan, *Makers of the Media Mind: Journalism Educators and Their Ideas* (Hillsdale, N.J.: Lawrence Erlbaum Associates, 1990), 95.

19. Edwin Emery and Henry Smith, *The Press in America* (New York:

Prentice-Hall, 1954). Smith was dropped as an author in the next seven editions, which were prepared by Edwin Emery and Michael Emery. A third author, Nancy L. Roberts, was involved in preparation of the book's last edition, which was published in 1996.

20. Histories of each of these technologies were published within twenty years of their emergence. David Brewster's 1856 publication, *The Stereoscope: Its History, Theory and Construction* (London: John Murray, Albermarle Street), was one of the earliest histories of one of the day's emerging photographic technologies; in 1860, sixteen years after Samuel Morse demonstrated America's first telegraph machine in 1844, George G. Prescott's *History, Theory, and Practice of the Electric Telegraph* (Boston: Ticknor and Fields) was published; Gleason Archer's history of radio appeared in 1936; and the first works on television appeared as early as the 1920s.

21. That year, for example, the American Telegraph Company published a thirty-six-page booklet titled *The American Telegraph Company and the New York Associated Press.*

22. Hudson, *Journalism in the United States,* 595.

23. Mason Jackson, *The Pictorial Press: Its Origins and Progress* (London: Hurst and Blackett, 1885); C. Thomas, "Illustrated Journalism," *Journal of the Society of Arts* 39 (January 30, 1891): 173ff; C. K. Shorter, "Illustrated Journalism: Its Past and Its Future," *Contemporary Review* 75 (1899): 481ff.

24. Raymond Fielding, *The American Newsreel, 1911–1972* (Norman: University of Oklahoma Press, 1972).

25. Marshall McLuhan, *Understanding Media: The Extensions of Man* (New York: McGraw-Hill, 1964).

26. Neil Postman, "The Reformed English Curriculum," in Alvin C. Eurich, ed., *Campus 1980: The Shape of the Future in American Secondary Education* (New York: Pitman Publishing, 1970), 160–68.

27. James W. Carey, *Communication as Culture: Essays on Media and Society* (Boston: Unwin Hyman, 1989).

28. Ibid., 35.

29. Carey and Quirk, "The Mythos of the Electronic Revolution," 114.

30. Raymond Williams and Ederyn Williams, eds., *Television: Technology and Cultural Form* (London: Routledge, 2003), 133.

31. Michael Schudson, *Discovering the News: A Social History of American Newspapers* (New York: Basic Books, 1978), 31.

32. Ibid., 35.

33. Menahem Blondheim, *News over the Wires: The Telegraph and the Flow of Public Information in America, 1844–1897* (Cambridge, Mass.: Harvard University Press, 1994).

34. Gwenyth L. Jackaway, *Media at War: Radio's Challenge to the Newspapers, 1924–1939* (Westport, Conn.: Praeger Publishers, 1995).

35. Robert W. McChesney, *Telecommunications, Mass Media, and Democracy: The Battle for the Control of U.S. Broadcasting, 1928–1935* (New York: Oxford University Press, 1994).

36. Kevin G. Barnhurst and John Nerone, *The Form of News: A History* (New York: Guilford Press, 2001), 8.

37. Ibid., 3.

38. Pablo J. Boczkowski, *Digitizing the News: Innovation in Online Newspapers* (Cambridge, Mass.: MIT Press), 3.

39. Mark Knights, *Representation and Misrepresentation in Later Stuart Britain: Partisanship and Political Culture* (Oxford and New York: Oxford University Press, 2005).

40. Anthony Smith and Richard Paterson, eds., *Television: An International History* (New York: Oxford University Press, 1995).

41. Mitchell Stephens, *A History of News: From the Drum to the Satellite* (New York: Penguin Books, 1988), 203.

42. Vint Cerf, "The Internet Is for Everyone," Internet Society, available at http://www.isoc.org/isoc/media/speeches/foreveryone.shtml (accessed on March 22, 2007).

43. John Naughton, *A Brief History of the Future: The Origins of the Internet* (London: Phoenix, 2000), 21–22.

44. Simon Hunt, "Dan Millman Interview," Spiritual Endeavors, available at http://www.spiritual-endeavors.org/basic/Dan_Millman.htm (accessed on March 26, 2007).

45. Robert J. Dowling and Paula Parisi, "Dialogue: Rupert Murdoch," *Hollywood Reporter,* November 14, 2005, available at http://www.hollywoodreporter.com/hr/search/article_display.jsp?vnu_content_id=1001479108 (accessed on April 16, 2007).

46. James W. Carey, "Journalism and Technology," *American Journalism* 7, no. 4 (Fall 2000): 129.

47. Brian Winston, "How Are Media Born?" in Michele Hilmes, ed., *Connections: A Broadcast History Reader* (Belmont, Calif.: Wadsworth Publishing, 2003), 3–17.

CHAPTER TWO

48. Anthony Barbieri-Low, "Wheeled Vehicles in the Chinese Bronze Age (c2000–741 B.C.)," *Sino-Platonic Papers* 99 (February 2000), available at http://www.sino-platonic.org.

49. Stephens, *A History of News,* 25.

50. Hazel Dicken-Garcia, *To Western Woods: The Breckinridge Family Moves to Kentucky in 1793* (Madison, N.J.: Fairleigh Dickinson University Press, 1991); Roy Alden Atwood, "Handwritten Newspapers," in Margaret A. Blanchard, ed., *History of the Mass Media in the United States: An Encyclopedia* (Chicago: Fitzroy Dearborn Publishers, 1998).

51. James Burke's book, *The Day the Universe Changed* (Boston and Toronto: Little, Brown, 1985), and its accompanying television program told the story of Gutenberg's press and its impact.

52. John Man, *Gutenberg: How One Man Remade the World with Words* (Hoboken, N.J.: John Wiley, 2002).

53. Norman E. Binns, *An Introduction to Historical Bibliography* (London: Association of Assistant Librarians, 1953), 39–91.

54. Elizabeth Eisenstein, *The Printing Revolution in Early Modern Europe* (Cambridge: Cambridge University Press, 1983), 91–94.

55. Margaret Spufford, *Small Books and Pleasant Histories: Popular Fiction and Its Readership in Seventeenth-Century England* (London: Methuen, 1981).

56. Rudolf Hirsch, "Printed Reports on the Early Discoveries and Their Reception," in Fredi Chiapelli, ed., *First Images of America: The Impact of the New World on the Old* (Berkeley: University of California Press, 1976), 2:537–38, esp. appendix 1, being a list of printed accounts of the New World.

57. Mitchell Stephens, "A History of Newspapers," for *Collier's*, available at http://www.nyu.edu/classes/stephens/Collier's%20page.htm.

58. Camillus Crivelli, "Periodical Literature—Mexico," available at http://www.newadvent.org/cathen/11685a.htm (accessed on April 16, 2007).

59. William S. Reese, "The First Hundred Years of Printing in British North America: Printers and Collectors," paper presented at the 1989 annual meeting of the American Antiquarian Society, available at http://www.reeseco.com/papers/first100.htm (accessed on April 17, 2007).

60. Sidney Kobre, *Development of American Journalism* (Dubuque, Iowa: W. C. Brown, 1969).

61. Massachusetts (Colony) Governor, "By the Governour and Council Whereas Some Have Lately Presumed to Print and Disperse a Pamphlet, Entitled, Publick Occurrences, Both Forreign and Domestick: Boston, Thursday, Septemb. 27th. 1690. Without the Least Privity or Countenance of Authority. The Governour and Council . . . Order That the Same Be Suppressed and Called In. . . ." (Boston: Printed by Bartholomew Green, September 29, 1690).

62. David Sloan, "John Campbell and the *Boston News-Letter*," available at http://www.earlyamerica.com/review/2005_winter_spring/john_campbell.htm.

63. *Boston News-Letter*, April 17–24, 1704.

64. Richard B. Keilbowicz, *News in the Mail: The Press, Post Office, and Public Information, 1700–1860s* (Westport, Conn.: Greenwood Press, 1989), 1.

65. *Boston News-Letter*, April 17–24, 1704.

66. Quoted in R. J. Brown, "Public Occurrences," available at http://www.historybuff.com/library/reffirstten.html (accessed on April 16, 2007).

67. Carol Sue Humphrey, *This Popular Engine: New England Newspapers during the American Revolution, 1775—1789* (Newark: University of Delaware Press, 1992).

68. Samuel Miller, *A Brief Retrospect of the Eighteenth Century* (New York: Printed by T. and J. Swords, 1803).

69. Alexis de Tocqueville, *Democracy in America* (Paris: C. Gosselin, 1836).

70. Ibid., chapter 5.

71. N. W. Ayer and Son, *N. W. Ayer and Son's American Newspaper Annual* (New York: N. W. Ayer and Son, 1897).

72. S. H. Steinberg, *Five Hundred Years of Printing,* new edition revised by John Trevitt (London: British Library, 1996), 139.

73. Ibid., 139–40, 148.

74. *New-York Spectator,* May 5, 1837.

75. John Clyde Oswald, *A History of Printing: Its Development through Five Hundred Years* (New York: D. Appleton, 1928), 344.

76. *Lowell (Mass.) Daily Citizen and News,* January 24, 1867.

77. *Cleveland Herald,* February 4, 1851.

78. *New York Sun,* January 29, 1851.

79. *Daily Evening Bulletin,* February 2, 1856.

80. *Daily Inter Ocean,* (Chicago), January 25, 1891.

81. *Milwaukee Journal,* July 17, 1893.

82. *Atchison Champion,* October 10, 1891.

83. *Daily Inter Ocean* (Chicago), May 19, 1893.

84. *St. Paul Daily News,* October 19, 1892.

85. Woody West, "How Electricity Came to Be: Its Innovators and Their Sparks," *Washington Times,* June 8, 2003, B06.

86. Quoted in *Daily National Intelligencer* (Washington, D.C.), May 10, 1837.

87. Frank Wicks, "The Blacksmith's Motor," *Mechanical Engineering,* July 1999.

88. Beaumont Newhall, *Photography: A Short Critical History* (New York: Museum of Modern Art, 1938).

89. John Tebbel and Mary Ellen Zuckerman, *The Magazine in America, 1741–1990* (New York: Oxford University Press, 1991); David Abrahamson, *Magazine-Made America: The Cultural Transformation of the Post-war Periodical* (Creskill, N.J.: Hampton Press, 1996).

90. Paul Heyer, *Titanic Legacy: Disaster as Media Event and Myth* (Westport, Conn.: Praeger Publishers, 1995), 5.

91. Raymond Fielding, *The American Newsreel, 1911–1967* (Norman: University of Oklahoma Press, 1972), 304.

92. Blondheim, *News over the Wires,* 53–55.

93. Erik Barnouw, *A Tower in Babel: The History of Broadcasting in the United States to 1933* (New York: Oxford University Press, 1966).

94. Ibid.

95. Quoted in John W. Murphy and John T. Pardeck, *Technology and Human Productivity: Challenges for the Future* (New York: Quorum Books, 1986), 149.

96. Smith and Paterson, *Television,* 41.

97. Ibid., 125.

98. Quoted in Thomas McCain and Leonard Shyles, eds., *The 1,000 Hour War: Communication in the Gulf* (Westport, Conn.: Greenwood Press, 1994), 69.

99. Quoted in Nicole Howard, *The Book: The Life Story of a Technology* (Westport, Conn.: Greenwood Press, 2005), 149.

100. Quoted in Jordan Raphael, "The New Face of Independent Journalism," *Online Journalism Review,* available at http://www.ojr.org/ojr/workplace/1017969538 (accessed on April 3, 2007).

101. Boczkowski, *Digitizing the News.*

102. Project for Excellence in Journalism, "The State of the News Media 2006: An Annual Report on American Journalism," available at http://www.stateofthenewsmedia.com/2006/index.asp (accessed on April 5, 2007).

103. Quoted in Herbert N. Casson, *The History of the Telephone* (Chicago: A. C. McClurg, 1922), 50.

104. Oliver Gramling, *AP: The Story of News* (New York: Farrar and Rinehart, 1940), 95.

105. Quoted in Stephen Kreis, "Lecture 4: The Medieval Synthesis and the Discovery of Man—The Renaissance," in *The History Guide: Lectures on Modern European Intellectual History,* 2000, available at http://www.historyguide.org/intellect/lecture4a.html (accessed on April 5, 2007).

106. Quoted in Thomas, *History of Printing,* 251–55.

107. Quoted in *Guardian,* August 29, 1993.

108. Quoted in "Grace Wyndham Goldie," available at http://www.terramedia.co.uk/quotations/Quotes_W.htm (accessed on April 5, 2007).

109. Quoted at http://www.terramedia.co.uk/quotations/Quotes_P .htm (accessed on April 5, 2007).

110. Quoted in William F. Baker and George Dessart, *Down the Tube: An Inside Account of the Failure of American Television* (New York: Basic Books, 1998), v.

111. Communication Act of 1934, ch. 652, §303.

112. George Gerbner, "Reclaiming Our Cultural Mythology," *In Context* 38 (Spring 1994): 40–42.

CHAPTER THREE

113. John E. Findling and Frank W. Thackeray, eds., *Events That Changed America in the Seventeenth Century* (Westport, Conn.: Greenwood Press, 2000), 48.

114. Dicken-Garcia, *To Western Woods,* 59–65.

115. Atwood, "Handwritten Newspapers."

116. Quoted in Hudson, *Journalism in the United States,* 119.

117. Douglas C. McMurtrie, *Wings for Words: The Story of Johann Gutenberg and His Invention of Printing* (New York and Chicago: Rand McNally, 1940), 277.

118. With the exception of Virginia's 50 percent literacy rate in the seventeenth century, which is cited by Harvey J. Graff, "Early Modern Literacies," in David Crowley and Paul Heyer, eds., *Communication in History: Technology, Culture, Society* (Boston: Allyn and Bacon, 2003), 113, the rest of these statistics are published in Lockridge's book, *Literacy in Colonial New England: An Enquiry into the Social Context of Literacy in the Early Modern West* (New York: W. W. Norton, 1974), 13.

119. Graff, "Early Modern Literacies," 111.

120. Ibid., 113.

121. John Ruston Pagan, *Anne Orthwood's Bastard: Sex and Law in Early Virginia* (New York: Oxford University Press, 2003), 15.

122. James J. Wilson, "Patronage of Printers," *True American,* January 19, 1807.

123. Howard [pseud.], "Domestic Economy," *National Advocate* (New York City), November 7, 1818.

124. Edwin Emery, Michael Emery, and Nancy Roberts, *The Press in America,* 9th ed. (Boston: Allyn and Bacon, 2000), 102.

125. Jerry Adler, "Hometown Paper Makes Good," *Newsweek,* August 13, 1984, 30.

126. Howard Kurtz, "A Bad Case of the '80s: Can a Once-Vital Newspaper Recover from the Age of Excess?" *Columbia Journalism Review* 31 (January-February 1993), available at http://archives.cjr.org/year/93/1/80s.asp (accessed on April 14, 2007).

127. David Bosse, *Civil War Newspaper Maps: A Cartobibliography of the Northern Daily Press* (Westport, Conn.: Greenwood Press, 1993), vii.

128. *New York Observer,* February 11, 1863; *New York Times,* February 9, 1863.

129. Quoted in Nancy Lewis and Richard Warrington Baldwin Lewis, *American Characters* (New Haven, Conn.: Yale University Press, 1999), 23.

130. Susan D. Moeller, *Shooting War: Photography and the American Experience of Combat* (New York: Basic Books, 1989), 25.

131. Daniel Defoe, *The Storm; or, A Collection of the Most Remarkable Casualties and Disasters Which Happen'd in the Late Dreadful Tempest, Both by Sea and Land* (London: Printed for G. Sawbridge and sold by J. Nutt, 1704).

132. Thomas Bennet Smith, "History of the Great Gale of Sept. 23, 1815 and of September 8, 1869," *Providence Evening Bulletin,* September 9, 1869.

133. Heyer, *Titanic Legacy,* 63.

134. Miguel Ramos and Paul S. Piper, "Web Waves: Tsunami Blogs Respond to Disasters," *Searcher* 13 (May 2005): 32.

135. Antone Gonsalves, "Bloggers, Citizen Journalists See Katrina from the Inside," InformationWeek, available at http://informationweek.com/story/showArticle.jhtml?articleID=170102810.

136. Quoted by J. C. Pinkerton in "The Riders of the Pony Express," available at http://www.authorsden.com/visit/viewarticle.asp?AuthorID=22173&id=14480 (accessed on April 14, 2007).

137. Moeller, *Shooting War,* 24.

138. Quoted in Harold Holzer, *Cooper Union* (New York: Simon and Schuster, 2004), 100.

CHAPTER FOUR

139. Mark Twain, *Following the Equator: A Journey around the World* (New York: P. F. Collier and Son, 1899), 75.

140. W. T. Coggeshall, *The Newspaper Record, Containing a Complete List of Newspapers and Periodicals in the United States, Canada and Great Britain* (Philadelphia: Lay and Brother, 1856), 147.

141. William Cronon, *Nature's Metropolis: Chicago and the Great West* (New York: W. W. Norton, 1991) 35.

142. *Minnesota Pioneer,* August 29, 1849, 1.

143. *Arrow,* April 29, 1892, 1.

144. James J. Hill, *Highways of Progress* (Garden City, N.Y.: Doubleday, Page, 1912), 235.

145. Quoted in Harold F. Peterson, "Some Colonization Projects of the Northern Pacific Railroad," *Minnesota History* (June 1929): 127.

146. Walter D. Kamphoefner, "German American Bilingualism: *Cui malo?* Mother Tongue and Socioeconomic Status among the Second Generation in 1940," *International Migration Review* 28, no. 4, special issue on "The New Second Generation" (Winter 1994): 846–64.

147. Ignatius Donnelly, *Minnesota: Address Delivered at the Broadway House, New York, on 27th March, 1857* (New York: Folger and Turner, Printers, 1857).

148. *County Call,* October 21, 1887.

149. Henry F. Mason, "County Seat Controversies in Southwestern Kansas," published on the Kansas State Historical Society Web site, available at http://www.kshs.org/publicat/khq/1933/33_1_mason.htm (accessed on April 14, 2007).

150. Quoted in Daniel Czitrom, *Media and the American Mind: From Morse to McLuhan* (Chapel Hill: University of North Carolina Press, 1982), 9.

151. Richard A. Schwarzlose, "The Nation's First Wire Service: Evidence Supporting a Footnote," *Journalism Quarterly* 62 (Winter 1980): 555.

152. *Newburyport (Mass.) Herald and Country Gazette,* February 21, 1800.

153. Quoted in Albert Bigelow Paine, *Mark Twain, a Biography: The*

Personal and Literary Life of Samuel Langhorne Clemens (New York and London: Harper and Brothers, 1912), 1:228.

154. Quoted in David Dary, *Red Blood and Black Ink: Journalism in the Old West* (New York: Alfred A. Knopf, 1998), 137. Dary included many stories like this one in this colorful book about frontier newspapers and their editors and readers.

155. Herbert Aptheker, *American Negro Slave Revolts* (New York: Columbia University Press, 1943), 162.

156. *New-York Evening Post,* September 23, 1800.

157. *Freedom's Journal,* April 13, 1827.

158. Daniel F. Littlefield and James S. Parins, *American Indian and Alaska Native Newspapers and Periodicals, 1826–1924* (Westport, Conn.: Greenwood Press, 1984), 1:xi.

159. Quoted in Philip S. Foner, *History of the Labor Movement in the United States* (New York: International Publishers, 1947), 1:230.

160. Quoted in "Women's History Quotations," National Women's History Museum, available at http://www.nmwh.org/Education/quotes.htm (accessed on April 7, 2007).

CHAPTER FIVE

161. Massachusetts (Colony) Governor, "By the Governour and Council," 1690.

162. *Pennsylvania Gazette,* October 2, 1729.

163. Quoted in L. Jesse Lemisch, ed., *Benjamin Franklin: The Autobiography and Other Writings* (New York: Penguin Group, 1961), 94.

164. Stephen Botein, "'Meer Mechanics' and an Open Press: The Business and Political Strategies of Colonial American Printers," *Perspectives in American History* 9 (1975): 127–225.

165. *Massachusetts Mercury,* January 1, 1793, 1.

166. *Charleston Mercury,* January 1, 1822, 1, 3.

167. Quoted in W. W. Story, *Life and Letters of Joseph Story* (Boston: C. C. Little and J. Brown, 1851), 127.

168. Quoted in Williams Brothers Publishers, *History of Ross and Highland Counties, Ohio* (Evansville, Ind.: Williams Brothers Publishers, 1880), 85.

169. *Virginia Gazette* (Williamsburg), April 30, 1737.

170. David A. Copeland, *Debating the Issues in Colonial Newspapers* (Westport, Conn.: Greenwood Press, 2000), x.

CHAPTER SIX

171. *Daily National Intelligencer,* May 28, 1844; *Ohio Observer,* May 30, 1844.

172. Quoted in Gerard J. Holzmann and Bjorn Pehrson, *The Early History of Data Networks,* available at http://www.spinroot.com/gerard/hist.html (accessed on April 14, 2007).

173. U.S. Congress, House, *Telegraphs for the United States,* H. Doc. 15, 25th Cong., 2d sess., 1837, 30.

174. *Rochester Daily American,* May 10, 1846.

175. U.S. Bureau of the Census, *Report of the Census for December 1, 1852* (Washington, D.C.: Robert Armstrong, 1853).

176. Hudson, *Journalism in the United States,* 480.

177. Victor Rosewater, *History of Cooperative Newsgathering in the United States* (New York: D. Appleton, 1930), 12–34. Until early in 2005, historians considered 1848 to be the year of the association's formation. In January 2005, the AP announced that a newly acquired collection of nineteenth-century documents revealed that the organization's origins were in 1846. See Richard Pyle, "19th-Century Papers Shed New Light on Origin of the Associated Press," available at http://www.ap.org/pages/about/whatsnew/wn_013106a.html (accessed on July 21, 2006).

178. James W. Carey, "Technology and Ideology," in his *Communication as Culture: Essays on Media and Society* (Boston: Unwin Hyman, 1989), 210.

179. David Mindich, *Just the Facts: How "Objectivity" Came to Define American Journalism* (New York: New York University Press, 1998), 64–94.

180. Christopher Scanlan, *Reporting and Writing Basics for the 21st Century* (New York: Oxford University Press, 2002).

181. Quoted in William Boddy, *New Media and Popular Imagination: Launching Radio, Television, and Digital Media in the United States* (New York: Oxford University Press, 2004), 20.

182. H. V. Kaltenborn, *Kaltenborn Edits the News* (New York: Gold Seal, 1937), iii, v.

183. "Radio-News Program in Final Stage," *Broadcasting,* February 1, 1934, 7.

CHAPTER SEVEN

184. Newhall, *Photography,* 76.

185. Arthur Mayger Hind, *An Introduction to a History of Woodcut* (1935, repr. New York: Dover, 1963); Douglas Percy Bliss, *A History of Wood-Engraving,* rev. ed. (London: Spring Books, 1964); A. Hyatt Mayor, *Prints and People: A Social History of Printed Pictures* (New York: Metropolitan Museum of Art, 1971).

186. Woodcut illustration (frontispiece and title page) from *An Affecting Narrative of the Captivity and Sufferings of Mrs. Mary Smith* (Providence, R.I.: L. Scott, 1815).

187. Lisa Mullikin Parcell, "Newspaper Illustrations," in W. David Sloan and Lisa Mulllikin Parcell, eds., *American Journalism: History, Principles, Practices* (Jefferson, N.C.: McFarland, 2002), 325–34.

188. Quoted in Maximillian E. Novak, *Daniel Defoe: Master of Fictions* (New York: Oxford University Press, 2003), 297.

189. *Pennsylvania Gazette,* June 6, 1745.

190. *Boston Gazette,* March 14, 1719.

191. Anon. [Benjamin Franklin], *Plain Truth, or, Serious Considerations on the Present State of the City of Philadelphia, and Province of Pennsylvania* (Pennsylvania: s.n., 1747).

192. Benjamin Franklin, *Autobiography* (New York: Penguin Classics, 1986), 182.

193. *Pennsylvania Gazette,* May 9, 1754.

194. The *Boston Gazette,* September 16, 1765, reported that the tree "upon which the Effigies of a Stamp Master was lately hung, was honour'd last Wednesday with the Name of, THE TREE OF LIBERTY."

195. Alice Sheppard, *Cartooning for Suffrage* (Albuquerque: University of New Mexico Press, 1994), 26–27.

196. *Frank Leslie's Illustrated Newspaper,* August 2, 1856.

197. William Cote and Roger Simpson, *Covering Violence: A Guide to*

Ethical Reporting about Victims and Trauma (New York: Columbia University Press, 2000), 130.

198. Kristine Brunovska Karnick, "NBC and the Innovation of Television News, 1945–1953," in Michele Hilmes, ed., *Connections: A Broadcast History Reader* (Belmont, Calif.: Wadsworth Publishing, 2003), 87.

199. "1968 in Television," available at http://en.wikipedia.org/wiki/1968_in_television (accessed on April 14, 2007).

200. Frank Beacham, "TV's Lost Technology," Spark Online, available at http://www.spark-online.com (accessed on April 14, 2007).

201. Quoted in Sean Mulcahy, "Convention 2000: With the CBS DGA Directing Team," *DGA Monthly,* available at http://www.dga.org/news/v25_4/feat_Demcon.php3 (accessed on April 14, 2007).

202. "City Council Hearing: Testimony of Lawrence Richette," Philadelphia Community Access Coalition, available at http://www.phillyaccess.org/hearings/1999–06–17_access/1999–06–17_lawrence_richette_36.html (accessed on April 14, 2007).

203. Sharon Strover, Museum of Broadcast Communications, "United States: Cable Television," available at http://www.museum.tv/archives/etv/U/htmlU/unitedstatesc/unitedstatesc.htm (accessed on April 14, 2007).

204. Television Digest, Inc., *Television Factbook* (Washington, D.C.: Television Digest, 1980–1981).

205. Bill Pierce, "Old Friends and New Equipment," *Digital Journalist,* available at http://www.digitaljournalist.org/issue9711/nutsandbolts9711.htm (accessed on April 14, 2007).

206. Dennis Dunleavy, "A Bird's View of History: The Digital Camera and the Ever-Changing Landscape of Photojournalism," *Digital Journalist,* February 2006, available at http://www.digitaljournalist.org/issue0602/dunleavy.html (accessed on April 14, 2007).

207. Dan Leonard, "A Snapshot of History: The Timeline of Digital Imaging," Timesonline, August 12, 2004, available at http://www.timesonline.co.uk/article/0,,16049–1213439,00.html (accessed on April 14, 2007).

208. See Digital Photography Review, available at http://www.dpreview.com/forums/forum.asp?forum=1026 (accessed on April 14, 2007).

209. Susan Sontag, *On Photography*, reprinted in David Crowley and Paul Heyer, eds., *Communication in History: Technology, Culture, Society* (Boston: Allyn and Bacon, 2003), 166–70.

CHAPTER EIGHT

210. Hiroshi Inose and John R. Pierce, *Information Technology and Civilization* (New York: W. H. Freeman, 1984), 3.

211. David Lyon, *The Silicon Society* (Grand Rapids, Mich.: Eerdmans, 1986), 13–14.

212. Diane Butler, *Future Work: Where to Find Tomorrow's High Tech Jobs Today* (New York: Holt, Rinehart and Winston, 1984), xiii.

213. Carey, *Communication as Culture*, 173–200.

214. Philip Meyer, *The New Precision Journalism* (Bloomington and Indianapolis: Indiana University Press, 1991).

215. Anon., (mission statement), November 15, 1999, National Institute for Computer-Assisted Reporting, available at http://www.nicar.org.

216. Paul Bissex, "The Web: Desktop Publishing Redux" available at http://www.well.com/~pb/cyb/arc/Cy.96.02.19.html (accessed on April 14, 2007).

217. David Carlson, "The Online Timeline," David Carlson's Virtual World, available at http://iml.jou.ufl.edu/carlson/timeline.shtml (accessed on April 14, 2007).

218. Barry M. Leiner, Vinton G. Cerf, David D. Clark, Robert E. Kahn, Leonard Kleinrock, Daniel D. Lynch, Jon Postel, Larry G. Roberts, and Stephen Wolff, "A Brief History of the Internet," Internet Society, available at http://www.isoc.org/internet/history/brief.shtml (accessed on April 14, 2007).

219. Kevin Kawamoto, *Digital Journalism: Emerging Media and the Changing Horizons of Journalism* (Lanham, Md.: Rowman and Littlefield, 2003), 2.

220. Patricia L. Dooley and Paul Grosswiler, "Turf Wars: Journalists, New Media and the Struggle for Control of Political News," *Harvard International Journal of Press and Politics* 2, no. 3 (1997): 34–37.

221. Marshall Ingwerson, "Electioneering Moves to a New State of the Art," *Christian Science Monitor,* November 4, 1992, 8.

222. Andrew Abbott, *The System of Professions: An Essay on the Division of Labor* (Chicago: University of Chicago Press, 1988), 92.

223. Quoted on Alex Chadwick's NPR *Day to Day* show, January 4, 2005, available at http://www.npr.org/templates/story/story.php?storyid=4258114.

224. Buzz Merritt, written statement to Les Anderson, Elliott School of Communication, Wichita State University, February 4, 2005.

225. Clifford Pugh, *Houston Chronicle,* July 29, 2004.

226. Mark Hamilton, "You Say Blogs . . . ," Notes from a Teacher, available at http://www.tamark.ca/students (accessed on April 14, 2007).

227. Tom McPhail, a University of Missouri journalism professor interviewed for a *USA Today* story, referred to in a Howard Kurtz *Washington Post* column, July 26, 2004.

228. *Pittsburgh Post-Gazette,* September 22, 2004.

229. *Denver Post,* September 26, 2004.

230. Quoted in David F. Gallagher, "Reporters Find New Outlet, and Concerns, in Web Logs," *New York Times,* September 23, 2002.

231. Patrick Sweeney, "GOP Blogger Served with Libel Lawsuit," *St. Paul Pioneer Press,* January 5, 2006, available at http://www.twincities.com/mld/pioneerpress/news/local/13551444.htm?template=contentModules/printstory.jsp (accessed on April 11, 2007).

232. Ibid.

233. Jeff Jarvis, "Should Mainstream Journalists Blog?" *Business Week Online,* July 30, 2005, available at http://www.businessweek.com/the_thread/blogspotting/archives/2005/07/should_mainstre.html (accessed on April 19, 2007).

234. Quoted in "New York Times Memo on Blogging," Cyberjournalist.net, available at http:www.cyberjournalist.net/news/003082.php (accessed on April 14, 2007).

235. "What Is This?" March 27, 2006, "Clicked Questions" column, MSNBC, available at http://www.msnbc.msn.com/id/6506550/#/Whatisthis.

236. Quoted in Xeni Jardin, "Podcasting Killed the Radio Star,"

Wired, available at http://wired.com/entertainment/music/news/ 2005/04/67344 (accessed on April 12, 2007).

237. Quoted in Roger Park, "The NY Times Front Page Podcast," available at http://www.imediaconnection.com/news/8138.asp (accessed on April 12, 2007).

238. Joe Strupp, "Mixing, Matching, and Multimedia," *Editor & Publisher* 139, no. 3 (March 23, 2006): 64.

239. Quoted in ibid.

240. Peter Schumacher, "User Feedback Drives Five Principles for Multimedia News on the Web," AUSC Annenberg Online Journalism Review, available at http://www.ojr.org/ojr/stories/050915schumacher (accessed on April 14, 2007).

CHAPTER NINE

241. Studies of popular icons such as the banjo and the automobile, as well as many other inanimate objects that have come to embody social and cultural meaning, have been published in journals in the field of communication and other areas of the humanities. See, for example, Wayne Shrubsall, "Banjo as Icon," *Journal of Popular Culture* 20 (1987): 31–59; Robert R. Kettler, "The Recalled Icon," *Indiana Social Studies Quarterly* 26 (1973–1974): 45–51.

242. *The Columbia World of Quotations,* Bacon quote available at http://www.bartleby.com/66/46/10546.html (accessed on April 14, 2007); Thoreau, *Yankee in Canada* (Montreal: Harvest House, 1853), 101; Nichols quote available at http://www.bartleby.com/66/55/41455.html (accessed on April 14, 2007).

243. Sidney A. Kimber, *The Story of an Old Press: An Account of the Hand Press Known as the Stephen Daye Press, upon Which Was Begun in 1638 the First Printing in British North America* (Cambridge, Mass.: The University Press, 1937), 5.

244. Ibid., 19.

245. Ibid.

246. Robert F. Roden, *Famous Presses: The Cambridge Press, 1638–1692—A History of the First Printing Press Established in English Amer-*

ica, Together with a Bibliographical List of the Issues of the Press (New York: Dodd, Mead, 1905), 1:9.

247. Thomas, *The History of Printing.*

248. Carl I. Wheat, *Pioneers: The Engaging Tale of Three Early California Printing Presses and Their Strange Adventures* (Published in the Pueblo of Los Angeles for the members of the Zamarano Club of Los Angeles and the Roxburghe Club of San Francisco, 1934).

249. Ibid., 3.

250. Ibid., 4.

251. Ibid., 5.

252. Ibid., 8 and 12.

253. Ibid., 14.

254. Quoted in ibid., 20.

255. American Antiquarian Society, *Old "No. 1": The Story of Isaiah Thomas and His Printing Press* (Worcester, Mass.: American Antiquarian Society, 1989).

256. "Elijah Parish Lovejoy," Altonweb: The River Bend, available at http://www.altonweb.com/history/lovejoy/ (accessed on April 14, 2007).

257. Ibid.

258. "A Short History of Alton," available at http://www.4sullivans .com/jtsgeneralstore/where.html (accessed on March 13, 2007).

259. Warren Upham and Rose B. Dunlap, *Minnesota Biographies, 1655–1912,* Minnesota Historical Society Collections, vol. 14 (St. Paul: Minnesota Historical Society, 1912), 171.

260. Richard Cordley, *A History of Lawrence, Kansas* (Lawrence, Kans.: E. F. Caldwell, 1895).

261. Quoted in G. Raymond Gaeddert, "First Newspapers in Kansas Counties, 1854–1864," *Kansas Historical Quarterly* 10 (February 1941): 19.

262. Douglas C. McMurtrie, *Jotham Meeker, Pioneer Printer of Kansas: With a Bibliography of the Known Issues of the Baptist Mission Press at Shawanoe, Stockbridge, and Ottawa, 1834–1854* (Chicago: Eyncourt Press, 1930); Katie Erickson, "Baptist Missionaries Were First to Arrive Here in 1830s," available at http://www.ottawaherald.com/ottawaguide/ 2000/baptist.html (accessed on April 6, 2007).

263. Jotham Meeker Papers, 1825–1864, Kansas State Historical Society, Topeka.

264. Quoted in ibid.

265. Legh Richmond Freeman and Douglas C. McMurtrie, *The History of the Frontier-Index (the "Press on Wheels"), the Ogden Freeman, the Inter-Mountains Freeman and the Union Freeman* (Evanston, Ill.: Butte City Union Freeman, 1883), 7.

266. Ibid., 8–9.

267. Kirke Mechem, "The Mystery of the Meeker Press," *Kansas Historical Quarterly* 4 (February 1935): 61–73.

268. Quoted in ibid., 63–64.

269. Quoted in ibid.

270. Ibid.

271. Ibid., 73.

272. Mary W. Berthel, *Horns of Thunder: The Life and Times of James M. Goodhue* (St. Paul: Minnesota Historical Society, 1948), 259–60.

273. Willougby Babcock, "The Goodhue Press," *Minnesota History Bulletin* 3 (February 1920): 291–94.

274. Paul R. Blankman, "Is It Really the Goodhue Press?" *Minnesota History* 56 (Fall 1999): 393–403.

275. The Quotations Page, available at http://www.quotationspage.com/quote/4861.html (accessed on February 24, 2007).

CHAPTER TEN

276. Henry David Thoreau, "Slavery in Massachusetts," in *The Writings of Henry David Thoreau* (Boston: Houghton Mifflin, 1906) 4:398.

277. Robert S. Mann, "Dailies Aided Greatly in Popularity of Broadcasting," *Editor & Publisher* (February 14, 1931): 34.

278. "AP and ANPA Declare War on Radio," *Broadcasting,* May 1, 1933, 5.

279. *Merriam-Webster's Online Dictionary,* available at http://www.m-w.com/cgi-bin/dictionary?va=blog (accessed on April 13, 2007).

280. Lex Alexander, "News-Record.com as Public Square," News-Record.com, available at http://blog.news-record.com/lexblog/archives/2005/01/newsrecordcom_a.html (accessed on April 15, 2007).

281. Quoted in Joan Konner, "It's the Content, Stupid," *Columbia Journalism Review* (November–December 1994), available at http://archives.cjr.org/year/94/6/pubnote.asp (accessed on April 15, 2007).

282. Fred Brown, "'Citizen' Journalism Is Not Professional Journalism," *Quill* 93, no. 6 (August 2005): 42.

BIBLIOGRAPHY

BOOKS

Banister, Jim. *Word of Mouse: The New Age of Networked Media.* Evanston, Ill.: Agate Publishing, 2004.

Barnhurst, Kevin G., and John Nerone. *The Form of News: A History.* New York: Guilford Press, 2001.

Bleyer, Willard G. *Main Currents in the History of American Journalism.* Boston: Houghton Mifflin, 1927.

Bliss, Douglas Percy. *A History of Wood-Engraving.* Rev. ed. London: Spring Books, 1964.

Bliven, Bruce, Jr. *The Wonderful Writing Machine.* New York: Random House, 1954.

Blondheim, Menahem. *News over the Wires: The Telegraph and the Flow of Public Information in America, 1844–1897.* Cambridge, Mass.: Harvard University Press, 1994.

Boczkowski, Pablo J. *Digitizing the News: Innovation in Online Newspapers.* Cambridge, Mass.: MIT Press, 2004.

Braun, Ernest, and Stuart MacDonald. *Revolution in Miniature: The History and Impact of Semiconductor Electronics.* Cambridge, Mass.: MIT Press, 1978.

Brennan, Bonnie, and Hanno Hardt, eds. *Picturing the Past: Media, History, and Photography.* Urbana and Chicago: University of Illinois Press, 1999.

Brewster, David. *The Stereoscope: Its History, Theory and Construction.* London: John Murray, Albermarle Street, 1856.

Brooks, John. *Telephone: The First Hundred Years.* New York: Harper and Row, 1976.

Carey, James W. *Communication as Culture: Essays on Media and Society.* Boston: Unwin Hyman, 1989.

Carter, Thomas Francis. *The Invention of Printing in China and Its Spread Westward.* New York: Columbia University Press, 1925.

Casson, Herbert N. *The History of the Telephone.* Chicago: A. C. McClurg, 1922.

Clark, Charles E. *The Public Prints: The Newspaper in Anglo-American Culture, 1665–1740.* Oxford: Oxford University Press, 1994.

Corn, Joseph J. *Imagining Tomorrow: History, Technology, and the American Future.* Cambridge, Mass.: MIT Press, 1986.

Cowen, Ruth Schwartz. *A Social History of American Technology.* New York: Oxford University Press, 1997.

Cutcliffe, Stephen H., and Terry S. Reynolds, eds. *Technology and American History.* Chicago: University of Chicago Press, 1977.

Czitrom, Daniel. *Media and the American Mind: From Morse to McLuhan.* Chapel Hill: University of North Carolina Press, 1982.

Dary, David. *Red Blood and Black Ink: Journalism in the Old West.* New York: Alfred A. Knopf, 1998.

Dicken-Garcia, Hazel. *To Western Woods: The Breckinridge Family Moves to Kentucky in 1793.* Madison, N.J.: Fairleigh Dickinson University Press, 1991.

Eisenstein, Elizabeth. *The Printing Revolution in Early Modern Europe.* Cambridge: Cambridge University Press, 1983.

Ellis, L. Ethan. *Newsprint: Producers, Publishers, Political Pressures.* New Brunswick, N.J.: Rutgers University Press, 1960.

Emery, Edwin, Michael Emery, and Nancy Roberts. *The Press in America.* 9th ed. Boston: Allyn and Bacon, 2000.

Fang, Irving E. *A History of Mass Communication: Six Information Revolutions.* Boston: Focal Press, 1997.

Fielding, Raymond. *The American Newsreel, 1911–1967.* Norman: University of Oklahoma Press, 1972.

Fisher, Claude S. *America Calling: A Social History of the Telephone to 1940.* Berkeley: University of California Press, 1992.

Foust, James C. *Online Journalism: Principles and Practices of News for the Web.* Scottsdale, Ariz.: Holcomb Hathaway, 2005.

Gillmor, Dan. *We the Media: Grassroots Journalism by the People, for the People.* Sebastopol, Calif.: O'Reilly, 2004.

Gitelman, Lisa, and Geoffrey B. Pingree. *New Media, 1740–1915.* Cambridge, Mass.: MIT Press, 2003.

Gramling, Oliver. *AP:The Story of News.* New York: Farrar and Rinehart, 1940.

Hilmes, Michele, ed. *Connections: A Broadcast History Reader.* Belmont, Calif.: Wadsworth Publishing, 2003.

Hind, Arthur Mayger. *An Introduction to a History of Woodcut.* 1935, repr. New York: Dover, 1963.

Hoe, Robert. *A Short History of the Printing Press.* New York: R. Hoe, 1902.

Hudson, Fredrick. *Journalism in the United States, from 1690–1872.* New York: Harper and Brothers, 1873.

Hudson, Heather E. *Communication Satellites: Their Development and Impact.* New York: Free Press, 1990.

Huss, Richard E. *The Development of Printers' Mechanical Typesetting Methods.* Charlottesville: University Press of Virginia, 1973.

Innis, Harold. *Empire and Communication.* Oxford: Clarendon Press, 1950.
———. *The Bias of Communication.* Toronto: University of Toronto Press, 1952.
———. *Changing Concepts of Time.* Toronto: University of Toronto Press, 1952.

Inose, Hiroshi, and John R. Pierce. *Information Technology and Civilization.* New York: W. H. Freeman, 1984.

Jackaway, Gwenyth L. *Media at War: Radio's Challenge to the Newspapers, 1924–1939.* Westport, Conn.: Praeger Publishers, 1995.

Jackson, Mason. *The Pictorial Press: Its Origins and Progress.* London: Hurst and Blackett, 1885.

Kawamoto, Kevin. *Digital Journalism: Emerging Media and the Changing Horizons of Journalism.* Lanham, Md.: Rowman and Littlefield, 2003.

Keenan, Thomas W., and Wendy Hui Kyong Chun, eds. *New Media, Old Media: A History and Theory Reader.* New York: Routledge, 2005.

Keirstead, Philip O. *Computers in Broadcast and Cable Newsrooms: Using Technology in Television News Production.* Mahway, N.J.: Lawrence Erlbaum Associates, 2005.

Kielbowicz, Richard B. *News in the Mail: The Press, Post Office, and Public Information, 1700–1860s.* Westport, Conn.: Greenwood Press, 1989.

Knights, Mark. *Representation and Misrepresentation in Later Stuart Britain: Partisanship and Political Culture.* Oxford and New York: Oxford University Press, 2005.

Lyon, David. *The Silicon Society.* Grand Rapids, Mich.: Eerdmans, 1986.

Mayor, A. Hyatt. *Prints and People: A Social History of Printed Pictures.* New York: Metropolitan Museum of Art, 1971.

McCain, Thomas, and Leonard Shyles, eds. *The 1,000 Hour War: Communication in the Gulf.* Westport, Conn.: Greenwood Press, 1994.

McLuhan, Marshall. *The Gutenberg Galaxy: The Making of Typographic Man.* Toronto: University of Toronto Press, 1962.

———.*Understanding Media: The Extensions of Man.* New York: McGraw-Hill, 1964.

McLuhan, Marshall, and Quentin Fiore. *The Medium Is the Message.* New York: Bantam Books, 1967.

McMurtrie, Douglas C. *Wings for Words: The Story of Johann Gutenberg and His Invention of Printing.* New York and Chicago: Rand McNally, 1940.

Mindich, David. *Just the Facts: How "Objectivity" Came to Define American Journalism.* New York: New York University Press, 1998.

Murphy, John W., and John T. Pardeck. *Technology and Human Productivity: Challenges for the Future.* New York: Quorum Books, 1986.

Naughton, John. *A Brief History of the Future: The Origins of the Internet.* London: Phoenix, 2000.

Newhall, Beaumont. *Photography: A Short Critical History.* New York: Museum of Modern Art, 1938.

Panzer, Mary, and Christian Caujolle. *Things as They Are: Photojournalism in Context since 1955.* New York: Aperture, 2006.

Prescott, George G. Prescott. *History, Theory, and Practice of the Electric Telegraph.* Boston: Ticknor and Fields, 1860.

Rosewater, Victor. *History of Cooperative Newsgathering in the United States.* New York: D. Appleton, 1930.

Schudson, Michael. *Discovering the News: A Social History of American Newspapers.* New York: Basic Books, 1981.

Schwarzlose, Richard A. *Nation's Newsbrokers.* Vol. 1, *The Formative Years: From Pretelegraph to 1865.* Evanston, Ill.: Northwestern University Press, 1989.

———. *Nation's Newsbrokers.* Vol. 2, *The Rush to Institution: From 1865 to 1920.* Evanston, Ill.: Northwestern University Press, 1990.

Sloan, W. David, and Lisa Mullikin Parcell, eds. *American Journalism: History, Principles, Practices.* Jefferson, N.C.: McFarland, 2002.

Smith, Anthony R., and Richard Paterson, eds. *Television: An International History.* New York: Oxford University Press, 1995.

Starr, Paul. *The Creation of the Media: Political Origins of Modern Communication.* New York: Basic Books, 2004.

Steinberg, S. H., revised by John Trevitt. *Five Hundred Years of Printing.* 4th ed. New Castle, Del.: Oak Knoll Press, 1996.

Stephens, Mitchell. *A History of News: From the Drum to the Satellite.* New York: Penguin Books, 1988.

———. *The Rise of the Image, the Fall of the Word.* New York: Oxford University Press, 1998.

Stevens, John D., and Hazel Dicken-Garcia. *Communication History.* Beverly Hills, Calif.: Sage, 1980.

Swan, Bradford F. *The Spread of Printing: Western Hemisphere—The Caribbean Area.* Amsterdam: Van Gendt, 1970.

Thomas, Isaiah. *The History of Printing in America, with a Biography of Printers.* 2nd ed. repr. New York: B. Franklin, 1967.

Williams, Raymond. *Harmful Myths: Television: Technology and Cultural Form.* New York: Oxford, 1978.

Williams, Raymond, and Ederyn Williams, eds. *Television: Technology and Cultural Form.* London: Routledge, 2003.

JOURNAL ARTICLES AND BOOK CHAPTERS

Atwood, Roy Alden. "Handwritten Newspapers." In Margaret A. Blanchard, ed., *History of the Mass Media in America: An Encyclopedia.* Chicago: Fitzroy Dearborn Publishers, 1998.

"Citizen Journalism." *Nieman Reports* 59, no. 4 (Winter 2005): 4–34. At http://www.nieman.harvard.edu/reports/05-4NRwinter/05-4NFwinter.pdf.

Dooley, Patricia L., and Paul Grosswiler. "Turf Wars: Journalists, New Media and the Struggle for Control of Political News." *Harvard International Journal of Press and Politics* 2, no. 3: 31–51.

Graff, Harvey J. "Early Modern Literacies." In David Crowley and Paul Heyer, eds., *Communication in History: Technology, Culture, Society,* *106–114*. Boston: Allyn and Bacon, 2003.

Jost, Kenneth. "Future of Newspapers: Will Print Papers Survive in an Online World?" *CQ Researcher* 16, no. 3 (January 20, 2006): 49–72.

"Journalism and Technology." Special issue of *American Journalism* 17, no. 4 (Fall 2000).

Shaw, Donald L. "At the Crossroads: Change and Continuity in American Press News, 1820–1860." *Journalism History* 8, no. 1 (Summer 1981): 35–50.

Shorter, C. K. "Illustrated Journalism: Its Past and Its Future." *Contemporary Review* 75 (1899): 481ff.

Thomas, C. "Illustrated Journalism." *Journal of the Society of Arts* 39 (January 30, 1891): 173ff.

Winston, Brian. "How Are Media Born?" In Michele Hilmes, ed., *Connections: A Broadcast History Reader,* 3–17. Belmont, Calif.: Wadsworth Publishing, 2003.

SELECTED NEWSPAPERS AND PERIODICAL ARTICLES

Brown, Fred. "'Citizen' Journalism Is Not Professional Journalism." *Quill* 93, no 6 (August 2005): 42.

Dunleavy, Dennis. "A Bird's View of History: The Digital Camera and the Ever-Changing Landscape of Photojournalism." *Digital Journalist,* February 2006, http://www.digitaljournalist.org/issue0602/dunleavy.html.

Edmonds, Rick. "As Blogs and Citizen Journalism Grow, Where's the News?" *Poynter Online,* November 14, 2005, http://www.poynter.org/content/content_view.asp?id=91391.

Konner, Joan. "It's the Content, Stupid." *Columbia Journalism Review,* November-December 1994, http://archives.cjr.org/year/94/6/pubnote.asp.

Pierce, Bill. "Old Friends and New Equipment." *Digital Journalist,* http://www.digitaljournalist.org/issue9711/nutsandbolts9711.htm.

DISSERTATIONS

Goble, George C. "The Obituary of a Machine: The Rise and Fall of Ottmar Mergenthaler's Linotype and U.S. Newspapers." Ph.D. diss., Indiana University, 1984.

INDEX

Patricia L. Dooley is professor of communication at Wichita State University and author of *Taking Their Political Place: Journalists and the Making of an Occupation* and *The Early National Period: Primary Documents on Events from 1800 to 1820.*

Neil Chase is the former editor of continuous news at the *New York Times,* the former deputy editor of news at the NYTimes.com, the former managing editor of CBS MarketWatch, and a former editor at the *San Francisco Chronicle* and the *Arizona Republic.*